YOUR SALES
CAREER GUIDE

DEDICATION

From David - As I sit here writing this dedication, I am 38,000 feet in the air. I spent the last 3 days meeting with executives from multiple companies to find solutions that could transform their businesses. I got to meet with multiple Chief Human Resource Officers, a Chief Operating Officer, and a multitude of other business leaders. It was a great week, and all the while my lovely wife was taking care of our 5-year-old, who I miss dearly. I love what I do, and I love my career, but I wouldn't be as happy as I am every day without them in my life.

I am writing this book for two reasons: First, to help people determine if sales is right for them, and second, to help the next generation of sales people get a leg up and successfully launch their careers. I truly want to give back to this group of young professionals, as so much of my success was catalyzed by the guidance I received early on. With that said, I want to recognize some of my mentors, leaders, and others who have helped shape my path greatly.

From Andy: This book is dedicated to those willing to work hard for the good of those around them. For those willing to take risks and get out of their comfort zone to better their lives. For the next generation of sales professionals who are going to further elevate the playing field.

ACKNOWLEDGEMENTS

From David and Andy: Hugh Barker – our developmental editor, thank you for helping us cleanup a bunch of our early messes in this book

Kelly Pierce – doing a ton of final edits, and adjusting the book so our target audience could read it easier. You have a very bright future ahead of you!

Everyone we surveyed – thank you for giving us the data and validation for a lot of our content to make sure our assumptions were correct, and even challenge some of our own beliefs.

Our shared friends, Scott Ingram, Jeff Bajorek, James Muir, and the entire Sales Success community, thank you for all the help and support

From David:

Ehrin Weiss – for all the late nights reading over my terrible writing and grammar to make this book read like it should.

Rob Cravaritis, who brought me into the world of professional selling, gave me my first chance at sales leadership, and took multiple chances on me - I will forever be grateful for how much you taught me about sales and business.

Gregory Donovan, an amazing leader and friend who taught me MEDDPICC and helped me elevate my game to new heights, thank you for challenging me to grow.

Jeff Walker, you have taught me so much about leadership and are truly one of the best people I have ever worked with. Thank you for your wisdom and your friendship.

From Andy:

At risk of inflating his already, erm, sizeable, ego, I have to thank David first, for being the first one to show me the light and get me interested in sales.

Rob Cravaritis – for giving me my first shot and spending time teaching the incredibly green rep that I was.

Huw Rothwell – for turning around and offering me an interview after I chased you for weeks on end after my first sales meeting with you

Jeremy Hill – for teaching me the ins and outs of agency recruitment and opening my eye to the human condition.

To my brothers and sisters in sales throughout the years: Amanda Tyner, Steve Scanlon, Travis Lane, Sofia Gonzalez, Nick Walker, AJ Mahmoud, Keith Smith, Sam Dunn, Moira Fraser, Gemma Cornish, Sara Loeb, Nico Sanguinetti, Kieran Scully, Talene Savadian, Vicka Krivokrasova, Alan Olivera, Taylor Wildman, Brandon Gambucci.

To Richard Vickers, Paulo Pontes, Bruno Stefani, Jay Tan, John Davies, Maxime Masraff, Alison Boob, Chris Olson, Cathy Sorsby, Todd Praisner, and Scott Van Horn for reasons known to each of them.

TABLE OF CONTENTS

PURPOSE

This is not a how-to-sell book. This book will help you determine if sales is right for you and, if so, equip you with the best practices to start and manage your career. So, why do people go in to sales? To help answer this question and supplement our own insights, we leveraged our network and asked hundreds of high-performing salespeople what led them to the profession. We learned a lot as we noticed common trends and patterns emerge. We heard many people say, "I wish I knew ten years ago what I know today!" This book will give you the inside scoop on what they know now. Our goal is to help you accelerate your learning and career.

The book is structured in an order that would follow your likely career decision process. First, ask yourself: do I even want to be a salesperson? Then, if you do, we will help you get that first job. Finally, once you're in, we'll teach you how to excel in your first months and years as a professional.

Of the hundreds of people we interviewed, we found four main reasons they chose to pursue a career in sales:

- I want to make a lot of **Money**
- I want **Freedom & Flexibility**
- I'm a **People Person**
- Someone **Recommended** it to me

Soon, we will address the myths of sales, what people love about sales, and what people hate about sales. But first, let's explore why people choose sales in the first place.

Money

Let's get real for a second—salespeople have the opportunity to be among the highest earners in ANY field. Now, this isn't true of every sales job, and it only truly comes into play if you are good at what you do, but sales differs from other career paths. Most jobs provide a base salary and maybe a bonus if your business does well. Salespeople have control of their own destinies, both in good times and bad. Low-performing salespeople will end up in the poorhouse, so it's very important to be good at your job. More on that later, after we have determined whether you have the core traits and basic skills to lead you to sales success. We can tell you right now that we've seen the highs and the lows, but we've also seen many people earn high six figures and low seven figures in sales. This level of success comes from many years of honing the craft and picking the right companies and products to sell, but few jobs match the long-term earning potential and low barriers of entry that sales has to offer.

Money is a great motivator, but please understand that we NEVER focus on the money we are going to make from a deal. Rather, we focus on solving the customer's problems. If we get paid to do that, so be it. Always put your clients first. Money-grubbing salespeople drive us crazy. You can make A LOT of money, but do it the right way and remain humble.

Freedom & Flexibility

Early on in your career, you might spend some or all your day in the office, or driving from tiny account to tiny account while you report your activity. However, this is temporary and purely for accountability until you have proven you have the discipline and motivation to go at it alone. Once you prove yourself, you'll be afforded the opportunity to work from home, from planes, trains, hotel rooms, and conference centers. We don't live in cubicles getting pounded by fluorescent lighting all day. We make our living both on the road, travelling to and from client meetings, and from the comfort of a carefully curated home office, complete with walls of books, our pets, and other personal touches. We aren't expected to be in the office, we're expected to be in front of people who want to buy from us. If we are in the office, it's to set more meetings or accomplish things we can't do from home. This gives our profession more freedom - and proportionately more responsibility - than almost any other. If you want a consistent, stable, low-pressure job where you stand around the water cooler and casually chat about the game last weekend, sales is not for you.

While this freedom has its appeal, it brings with it a bit of natural loneliness. It's great to do what you want when you want, but at times, you will feel like you are on an island. Freedom is one of the top reasons for being in sales, but it comes with an inherent lack of deep, meaningful relationships with co-workers and others. Since you will may be mostly traveling or working from home, many long-term relationships will be virtual ones. Before choosing a remote position, it's important to understand that the freedom is a double-edged sword.

People Person

The idea that a salesperson has to be a "people person" is both a myth and a reality. The myth is that it's a prerequisite trait. The reality is that, if you like talking to people and naturally seek out new conversations, it will be easier to pick up the phone and talk to people.

Being a "people-person" is what motivates many to go into sales. If that's your starting point, you'll soon realize that you actually HATE people! We're joking... but there's a serious point here- sales really can show you the most difficult sides of people. Consider this: people will lie to you, cancel meetings at the last minute (or just now show up), waste your time, and otherwise negatively impact your ability to make money and achieve your goals. Everyone has their own agenda, both inside your company at your prospects and clients. This makes navigating relationships very important. A people person will have a knack for this, but everyone will get frustrated from time to time.

> *From David - I remember a job I applied for right out of college: they asked everyone to take a personality assessment. In the test, I ranked very high for 'trusting people'. That was the actual reason they turned me down for the job, and I can see why. Salespeople always need to be challenging other people to make changes, and to buck the status quo. If you are a people person, sometimes you just want people to "like" you. You need to understand that this desire can create challenges of its own.*

Someone Recommended It to Me

If a successful salesperson has told you that you'd be good at it, then AWESOME! If someone suggests it as a career, but they have never sold a thing in their life, well just saying.

Think about it. Would you take career advice from someone who has never done that career? We aren't trying to discourage you, but we can't tell you how often we have interviewed someone and asked, "So why sales?" and the answer is "I am a people person, so my friend said I should be in sales…"

It's great if you are thinking about sales, but choose your path intentionally, with eyes wide open.

SECTION 1 – SO YOU ARE CONSIDERING A CAREER IN SALES?

HOW DID WE GET IN TO SALES?

Sales isn't for everyone, but it's a more reasonable career path than many realize. It isn't a manipulation game, like some assume. Instead, it's a problem-solver's paradise, a puzzle master's playground, and a creative-thinker's sandbox. If you like finding creative solutions to problems, you might like sales more than you'd ever imagine.

From Andy - Before I even considered a career in sales, I told myself things like, "I'm not that social, I'd rather listen than speak in group conversations. I'm not comfortable talking to strangers. I've never even played a round of golf in my life ..." So, there I was - I'd graduated college and had been working for a good firm for three years in a training-rotational role. The trouble was that my work wasn't fulfilling and I wasn't happy. I took stock of my situation and trajectory and realized that I didn't really care for the path I was on. I had no passion for the industry I was in, I wasn't a great culture fit for the company, and at the time, providing sales support for something I didn't particularly care about didn't excite me. (Shocking, I know.)

The economy had finally begun to recover from the 2008 crash, so there were opportunities out there. The trouble was that I simply didn't know what was out there. I reached out to family and friends and tried to figure out what to do next. Luckily, one of the people I reached out to was my friend, David Weiss, who knew me better than I knew myself. He'd gone straight into sales and was able to help me see the light, so to speak. What I found once I started was very different from my preconceptions.

Sales isn't about glad-handing and delivering snazzy presentations. It involves working diligently day-in and day-out, taking strategic breaks to think, analyze what's working and what isn't, and make improvements to processes based on real world experience. As a result, it's also about solving problems for people and delivering revenue, profit, jobs, and growth to your company as a result.

From David: I clearly remember the day when my parents told me I needed to get a job. I was 16 years old, an average high school kid home for the summer. I had plans, big plans: you know, the usual hanging out with friends, causing trouble, playing video games ... generally fun, but unproductive summer things. Frankly, I think my parents were scared to leave me with a significant amount of unstructured time and I can't say I blame them. It's funny how quickly my life changed in that moment, and how unhappy I was about my parents ruining my brilliant summer plans. Like many people my age, I had aspirations of spending time at the beach and hanging out with friends, but like many events in life, you need to wait to see the effect many years down the road to really determine the true impact. Not to overshare, but I am a bit of a nerd. I was into computers in a big way and a bit of a troublemaker - an unusual combination, I know. This was when you got your internet delivered to you on 3.5" floppy discs in the mail from a company called AOL, when dial-up was still a 'thing'. I still can hear the screeching of the modem.

Figuring out how to get computers to do cool things came naturally to me, and so did building them. I used to frequent

7

a local PC store in my town. On that day, I walked in and spoke with the owner, Hy Vu, as I often did. I told him how my summer plans had been squashed by my parents and that I needed to get a job. I was fortunate that I had this passion and relationship with Hy. He offered me a job on the spot, starting off by building and fixing computers. I did this for about month, and I soon realized I was having a blast after all. I was making decent money and hanging out with people who shared similar interests - I was even starting to think I might become an engineer. Then, just by chance, I was speaking with a customer in the store about a computer I had finished building. Another customer overheard our conversation and asked me some questions. My first referral came when the customer I was working with recommended my work. I started working with the new customer, asked them what they wanted, and through my technical expertise helped them design a computer that they wanted to buy. My first sale: it felt awesome!

Hy approached me after the client left, asked if I wanted to do that more often, and offered me a piece of every sale. I thought: "why not, it'll be more money, I can talk to people, help them get the right solution, and build it for them." Sounded like fun to me.

Welcome to sales, David…

MYTHBUSTING – WHAT SALES IS AND WHAT SALES ISN'T

What comes to mind when you think of a salesperson? Jane is sitting at her computer doing research, writing emails, having internal meetings about product scope, functionality, and roadmap, all while creating business cases to drive organizational change, considering each stakeholder that will be impacted by the project she's proposing. Jack is a stressed and overworked guy in a cheap, ill-fitted suit, who gives bone-crushing handshake, trying to aggressively push product. Who seems more like your idea of a salesperson? Depending on your level of sales experience, you might be surprised that Jane is what you'll find top-level professional salespeople doing day in and day out, while Jack is the type of guy we all kind of feel sorry for.

In this section, we'll be examining and defining what sales is, what sales isn't (or shouldn't be, at least), and what to expect from a sales position. But before we do that, let's cover the most common myths about sales:

1. Salespeople are tricksters to be feared

2. Sales is easy - good products sell themselves

3. You must be extroverted to succeed in sales

4. Sales is not a feasible long-term career

5. Salespeople are selfish and only care about themselves

6. You need a business background to be in sales

Myth 1 – Salespeople are tricksters to be feared.

Reality – this may be the oldest and most common misconception in the book. It probably goes back to the cliché of the "used car" salesman and the stigma it carries. If you think that sales is about nothing more than putting money in your pocket at all costs, don't become a salesperson. Don't give the profession a bad name – go do something else. Salespeople are agents of change. In the business world, without sales, no significant change can occur.

It's likely that anyone considering a sales career knows this misconception still haunts our profession. You can only change this perception by being informed and being an expert in what you are selling. You need to ask questions BEFORE you present solutions and make sure you are putting your client's needs above your own. We promise, if you do that, not only will your needs be fulfilled, you'll develop long-term partnerships and people who will seek you out to do business with you or refer their peers to you.

Myth 2 – Sales is easy - good products sell themselves.

Reality – we would argue sales is one of the most difficult and rewarding jobs there is. What makes it difficult? Go try and get anyone to change anything they are doing. In fact, try and change something YOU are doing on any consistent basis. Seriously, try waking up 30 minutes earlier every day for the next month to work out. It's a good idea - it would lead to obvious improvements in your health and life, but we bet you won't. Why? Because change is HARD, and you may not fully accept or internalize the reason for making change.

Let's say we told you that working out 30 minutes a day would make you live longer, be more productive, have more energy, and be more attractive. Would you make the change? Probably not. Why? Because you knew that already. We all know that there are things we could be doing differently, doing better, that would lead to a better, healthier life. And yet, most of us aren't doing all these things that would lead to better, healthier, happy lives.

You know what would get you to make a change? You would need to think about your life objectives and find some way to tie them to the idea that working out could help you achieve them. You would need to make the choice and see how it helps you accomplish that objective, something that meant more to you than 30 minutes of sleep. That's the business case for change. Sales almost always relies on a reason to change, a pathway to achieve a better outcome, and the ability to go down that path. Something that the person you are selling to believes. It can be extremely hard to get someone to see that reason and path, especially if they aren't looking for it. It might be easy if a customer knocked on your door and said, "I need help." But that is rarely the case. And even when it happens, if they knocked on your door, they're probably knocking on your competitor's door and asking the same questions.

This exact challenge is why a sales career provides an endlessly rewarding career opportunity. But it will only be rewarding if you like helping people solve problems they didn't know they had and then getting to see the fruits of your labor.

How cool would it be if you could get someone to wake up 30 minutes earlier, they became more productive, and as a result, they got a big promotion at work? Sales is all about helping people see a reason for change, facilitating the change, and helping them achieve a better result. What could be more exciting than that?

Myth 3 – You must be extroverted to be in sales.

Reality – People who have the "gift of gab" and are extroverted talk to and engage more people, so they're better equipped to navigate complex social interactions. This may make them appear to be better suited for a profession that requires many conversations.

However, there is a more complicated side to this. Sales is about seeking out information with the purpose of understanding a potential need for change, and then facilitating that change with your product or service. It may require more energy for an introverted person to start the conversation, but once the conversation has started, you are simply asking questions to understand a prospect's needs. Sales Engineer roles, or any technical-based selling role, are often a great match for an introvert's natural skills. The initial prospecting outreach, while conversational, has incredibly deep roots in science and psychology and can be applied in a very methodical way that play to an introvert's strengths. We have seen people of all personality types be successful. Sales is highly process driven, so if you learn a successful process and repeat it, anyone can find success. In this book, we will talk about how some of those personalities play out. What's important is that you have an innate curiosity to learn, solve problems, and work with people towards positive change. If you do, sales is for you. You will just need to learn to play to your strengths and find ways to support those activities that may not come naturally.

Myth 4 – Sales is not a good long-term career.

Reality – we will discuss this a few times, because at its core, this book is about why sales *is* a good long-term career and how to see if it makes sense for you. Let's be clear: a successful sales career can take you places few careers could. The potential for long-term growth, financial freedom, and career path flexibility is far greater than the majority of career paths. Looking down the road, you have a few options: You could exclusively build a career as an individual contributor with increasing levels of growth, after which you might pivot into sales management and leadership, then, if you're lucky enough, you could eventually own all sales processes and direct the personnel in a business. This is a common career path. Many sales leaders are groomed to be CEOs. You can also go into sales training or even start your own company.

As the foundation for business, very few jobs prepare you for long-term success like sales. Sales forces you to wear many hats: you need to be an entrepreneur who's willing to take risks, a finance person getting exposure to profit, margins, profit *& loss statements. You'll gain experience as an operations person, seeing how things really happen once the sale is made and your organization needs to deliver service. You will also touch on implementation, customer service, customer success, etc. Salespeople are THE business drivers: nothing happens without them, and this provides business exposure and opportunities for growth like no other role.

We are the navy seals of the business world: give us a mission and we find a way to accomplish it. No other career or position in a business operates like that. But this does mean it is a complex role, so bear in mind that you're not signing up for a run-of-the-mill 9 to 5.

Myth 5 – Salespeople are selfish and only care about themselves.

Reality – Hey look, people are generally selfish at their core. Most folks are primarily focused on self-preservation. But if you're only looking out for yourself, you won't last long in sales. Your clients will see it, your colleagues will see it, and it will be reflected in your results. People won't buy from you if they sense you are just doing it to make money from them. In fact, nothing turns people off more than saying you have a deadline, or that you have a number to hit, or talking about how much money you will make from them buying your product.

No one cares about you, and we mean that in the nicest way possible. People care about themselves and what you can do for them. If you show that you also care about them, that you can help, and that you are serving their interests, you will go far. The sales leader board is very transparent: few careers are measured so clearly. Your success and your failure is posted everywhere for people within your own company to see. But when it comes to the client, make it about how you can help them achieve their goals, and they will help you achieve yours.

Myth 6 – You need a business background to be in sales.

Reality – Business acumen is valuable, but it can be learned on the job. Sales is a skillset in and of itself, rarely learned outside of the sales environment. We've met former professional engineers, professional chefs, and HR Managers who've transitioned to sales and have become wildly successful. One of the keys to sales success is an "always be learning" mentality. The best salespeople are constant readers. They are highly critical of themselves and constantly seek to improve their craft. Having said that, good business people make great salespeople. If that's not your background, it is something you need to focus on from the start. A strong background in sales is often a foundation for people who go on to become CEOs and senior business leaders. The good news is, there is a long path between where you are today and becoming a future leader of the free world. You can learn everything you need to know - just be aware that as you grow your sales muscles, you'll also be growing business muscles.

DEFINING SALES

Now that we know what sales is and isn't, how should we define sales in technical terms? According to Google, sales is "the exchange of a commodity for money; the action of selling something." This is a very business-to-consumer (B2C)-oriented definition, which often involves a commodity-driven transaction.

A B2B Definition of Sales

The definition above is technically correct but didn't anyone tell Google you can't use the word in the thing you are trying to define? Let's really dig in to what sales is in more depth, focusing specifically on business-to-business sales.

Sales has changed greatly in recent years. In the past, we were trained to tell people everything about the product and all the features, benefits, reasons to buy, and so on... Now, thanks to the internet, buyers are more informed than ever. Everyone you speak to has the ability to do their own research, either long before you meet or right after you leave. This shift in buyer behavior has created the need for a different set of required skills. So how about this for a definition:

Sales is the process of seeking out information from people with the purpose of helping them to make positive changes using your product or service.

To be successful at sales, it helps to be a naturally curious person. This will help you direct your conversations with clients to understand what they are doing, what their current state is, what improvement they are looking for, and how you can help them get to the desired future state.

The better you are at this process of finding the right people to talk to, the greater the depth of your conversations, and the more strongly you can align your solution with the challenge at hand, the greater your likelihood of success.

Later, we will talk about developing a successful sales process. But for now, think of sales as the process of finding information to help people make a positive change with your product or service.

WHAT DO PEOPLE LOVE ABOUT SALES?

There's a lot to love about a career in sales. Here are some examples:

When we surveyed hundreds of high-performing sales people, freedom came back as one of the best perks of a sales career. It may not be there from day one for everyone, but over time, sales offers more freedom than most professions. You often get to set your own schedule, your work is measured in output, not hours, and you are not chained to a cubicle for your entire career. We get the privilege of extreme ownership, of acting like a business owner and building our own franchise inside of a larger business.

We are the world's problem solvers. Without us, our clients don't know how much better things can be. Offering solutions that improve outcomes can be extremely rewarding. Imagine for a second that you met with an executive, helped them diagnose areas that they wanted to improve, and through your solutions, their business saw millions of dollars in new revenue. What's more, the person you worked with probably got positive recognition within their business. Maybe they got a promotion or a sizeable bonus. If so, you just personally helped that person and their family move forward in their lives.

We drive businesses forward - sales make things happen. In a way, everyone else in a business works for us: if we aren't selling, the business will collapse, and no one will have jobs. We are rewarded well for our efforts with significant sums of money, trips, perks, concert tickets, car allowances, and sizeable expense accounts to treat clients to dinners and entertainment. We are the front line. We see the changes in the landscape before anyone else and this gives us the ability to see around the corner and provide valuable insight to the business on its future.

We are the agents of change. We truly transform how people and businesses operate—THAT IS EXCITING! No other profession has that type of impact. Through these actions, you build customers for life and constantly help businesses and clients grow. You always know where you stand and when you are ahead of the game - it's one of the best feelings you can get professionally. Your name is in lights. Everyone wants to be your friend and to learn from you. People in the business will come to learn ways of replicating your success.

The feeling you get from successfully closing deals in sales is amazing. To win, you had to find new solutions and make businesses better. Imagine you worked for months, or even years on a deal: countless meetings, hundreds of emails and phone calls, internal politics, contract negotiations, and YOU found a way to win, all while competing against other salespeople and companies. It's like training for the Olympics and taking home the gold!

There was an article recently published that discussed the career paths and lives of multi-millionaires and billionaires ("The No. 1 Job Billionaires and Multimillionaires Held Before They Got Filthy Rich" on Marketwatch.com). The author surveyed 45 people, 66% of whom had a background in sales and credited that experience for their accomplishments. Tech billionaires Mark Cuban (current CEO of the Dallas Mavericks, among other things), Michael Dell (yes, that Dell), Larry Ellison (Oracle), and Reed Hastings (CEO of Netflix) all got their start in sales. The list goes on.

As this shows, a career in sales can open many lucrative doors.

WHAT DO PEOPLE HATE ABOUT SALES?

When someone is on top, someone must be on the bottom, and this truly sucks. There will always be times when you are that person. When you get behind, it's hard to catch up and easy to get down on yourself. Sales is not for the faint-hearted. In fact, it can be one of the most stressful jobs you can have. You may have been on top last year, but there is always this "What have you done for us lately?" question hanging over your head. "So what, you hit goal last month? What about this month?" That is ever-present. You always need to be working for tomorrow and staying ahead of the game. It's the flip side of the things people love about sales: when things aren't going well everyone can see it. It is a very transparent profession. Your metrics, goals and achievements (or lack thereof) are always visible - you can never hide. Because of this, sales never can or will be a 9–5 job. You can develop the feeling that you always need to work, since the more you work, the more money you make. You want a raise, so you make more calls, go on more appointments, and close more business. Be careful – if you're doing more for too long, you can burn yourself out fast.

Another interesting aspect of sales is the way it can change your perception. You can perceive that you are being used, lied to, and otherwise manipulated for others' gain. Some people want advice, others better pricing in their deal, but when you no longer have something to offer, people disappear. This can make it hard to know where you stand with people, or who your real friends are.

Our absolute favorite thing about sales is also the thing that we both absolutely hate about it – the work never ends. You can always do more. There's never a situation where you can honestly look at your day and tell yourself "You know, I've done enough. There's really nothing else I can do today to move the needle. I can kick back, kill some time, and wait until my manager gives me an assignment." It's great because you'll never have a lull, but it can be rough because it feels like the pressure is always on. In the early stages of a sales career, it can be difficult to look back at your day, week, or month and feel you've accomplished something without feeling worried or guilty. It's not uncommon to have a little voice in the back of your head saying, "You know you could have done more - why didn't you? You could have gotten to work earlier, spent less time chatting, made that personal call after hours, etc." However, as time goes on and you get a feel for your skills, process, and goals, you'll develop a sense of how much work you need to be doing in a given day and you'll learn to manage this stress. Remember this:

Your WORST day and your BEST day could be the SAME day!

That saying really captures the unpredictable nature of our profession. In other jobs you have highs and lows, but in no other profession are they so pronounced and unpredictable. For instance, if a chef undercooks food, or an accountant messes up an Excel formula and sends out a bad report, their days will take a bad turn because they messed something up. But in sales, you can do everything right and still have terrible results some days. These constant ups and downs can put professional sellers on emotional rollercoasters on a daily basis.

From David - Here's a story from my early days of selling about not taking things personally. I had just told my girlfriend, and future wife, that we could no longer go to her favorite Sushi restaurant—the only decent one in Rochester NY—and she LOVES Sushi ... At this time in my career, I was working for ARAMARK selling uniforms and ancillary products like floor mats, bar and shop towels, and so on ... it wasn't the most glamorous work, but being the eager young salesperson, I was, I tried to sell to everyone.

I had always been told if someone likes you and trusts you, they will buy from you. I generally believed that and still do to a point. However, I quickly realized that nothing was a sure thing. At that point of my sales career, I was still green and took things very personally. So when I felt someone was going to buy from me, and they didn't, I would personally stop using their business. I still felt as if they had personally rejected me, rather than the solution I was offering. That's exactly what happened with the sushi restaurant I boycotted.

I know ... don't judge me. I was a silly kid back then. I am grateful my now wife chose to stay with me. She made a point very clearly that I was no longer allowed to sell to places she liked to go, but that is not the point of this story.

As we've mentioned, this life we have chosen is ranked among the most stressful jobs you can have. It requires thick skin, grit, persistence, perseverance, and all types of mental and physical toughness.

The life of a salesperson is akin to riding a rollercoaster. I remember one particularly devastating low after I lost a deal with a Fortune 100 company. This company was looking for multiple providers to help support their growth - the deal was valued well into seven figures. Someone could've lived off that commission for quite some time. I was ecstatic when they told us that we were selected as a vendor. Only one hurdle was left: legal terms that we were assured wouldn't be an issue. I was elated, but by that point in my career I had at least learned to be cautious. Ten years earlier, my younger self might have gone right out and bought a new car expecting a win.

As we sifted through the legal language one term leaped out at us that we simply would not be able to get past. I can't share all the details here for obvious reasons, but I was devastated.

At least I didn't decide to stop doing business with that company. I consider that growth. It only took 10 years!

Just another day in the life. Of course, these situations don't happen every day, and this was a particularly bad loss. But these things will happen. Most losses won't feel as catastrophic, and you can't win them all. You will get verbal agreements on deals that don't pan out in the end. You will get to the contract stage and have legal issues. You will get to the implementation stage, something will go awry, and the client will pull out of the deal. There are many areas of risk in our profession, so it's important to know what you're getting into.

If you choose this path, be prepared for frequent ups and downs. Learn not to take losses personally and don't be afraid to ask for help emotionally, physically, and spiritually. We've been able to cope with the trials thus far; maybe we're lucky, maybe we have a keen awareness of our shortcomings, or for David, maybe it's because he married a psychologist.

The serious point is that this is not a job you should go at alone. The rewards can be great, but with all reward there is risk and potential hardship. This profession is not for the thin-skinned or weak-willed. It's important to have a strong support system. You will be riding a hell of a rollercoaster, and just at the point when you hit your goals, the year will reset and the "What have you done for us lately?" begins again.

DNA OF A SALES ALL-STAR

If you score highly in the traits in this section there is a higher chance of you being suited to a career in sales. You can be successful without these traits, but it will be harder. The more closely the required skills of the job align with your innate tendencies, the happier you will be, and the faster you will find success.

Agency- The ability to act independently, make choices, and frankly, get shit done. Certain people, no matter the obstacles and challenges in front of them, no matter the setbacks they encounter, always seem to accomplish their goals one way or another. These people have a high level of agency.

Grit- The ability and willingness to persevere through adversity to achieve your goals. Long term success in sales is an exercise in failing repeatedly yet successfully. In the B2B world, great sales people only win a fraction of the deals they get into – they lose far more than they win. But they keep going, motivated from their losses, determined to achieve their goals.

Urgency—The natural drive to move things along quickly and make things happen sooner than they would without your intervention. If you have a high sense of urgency, you become uncomfortable when progress isn't made and it will drive you to take positive action. Imagine you have one year to hit your sales targets, but your deals take six months to a year to close. That means that on day one of a new year, you are potentially behind your sales target, meaning you need to build a targeted list of people, engage in prospecting efforts to find them, follow up with them, gain access, run a sales process, and drive for a signature. People with high urgency block time on their calendar to build lists and get these things done quickly. They follow up on a weekly basis with messages that call for responses including business cases and proposed meeting dates. When told to wait, change dates, or that there is no budget, they take those objections and overcome them quickly, finding ways to earn the business. Without urgency, dates slip, years are missed by weeks and months, and some things never happen. Urgency keeps you going, moves you forward, increases your activity, and accelerates your success.

Assertiveness—Being self-assured or confident (without being needlessly or overly aggressive.) Salespeople are agents of change. If you speak your mind, take charge, and enjoy persuading others towards your opinions, you have natural traits of assertiveness. Salespeople are business leaders. Our job is to seek out areas that need change and get others to get on board with making those changes. If you don't have a degree of natural assertiveness, then when someone disagrees with you, says they are not interested, or tries to tell you that you are wrong, you may back down and agree.

Creativity—Do you like to create something from nothing? Do you imagine better ways of doing things and enjoy helping other people align with that vision? Salespeople need to be able to look at a problem within a business (even within your own solution) and imagine a different way of doing things. We can't tell you how many times we have created new solutions within our company's products, at one-point when we were selling advertising solutions together, and we created sponsorships for an event we were hosting. We had music sponsors, bag sponsors, bar sponsors… if it made sense, we made and sold a sponsorship for it. We almost doubled the revenue of the event by creating sponsorships where none existed before. A client's needs and your products aren't always perfect square holes and square pegs – you need to get creative to figure out how to make something work that can and should work. Sure, sometimes it works that way. But often, your product may only do a certain percentage of what the client needs, or is willing to buy. In this case, if you could tweak something here or there, or inspire the client to rethink their needs, you may be able to solve 100% of the problem at hand. This requires a creative mind that knows how to re-engineer the solution or frame the problem in a different light.

Competitive— A competitive person regularly tests themselves - against their peers or themselves, to understand how good they are or aren't, and to uncover what they need to do to get better. Then they work on that and test themselves again. It's well known that many companies and sales leaders prefer to hire former high-level athletes. In order to compete at a high level, an athlete has to have worked incredibly hard and diligently to improve every little aspect of their performance. It's a relentless pursuit of competing against your former self, making sure you're always better. Top performing athletes and sales people don't make the same mistakes twice – when they make a mistake, they learn from it and move on.

Empathy—A large part of sales is understanding another person's point of view, seeing why things are done the way they are done, and finding ways to help someone personally and professionally make changes that show measurable improvement. One of the main ways you do this is by asking a lot of questions and putting yourself in other people's shoes. This requires a high degree of empathy, which enables you to relate and demonstrate how what you are bringing to the table will really help them (rather than just helping you).

Curiosity— Do you love to ask why? And then, when someone gives you an answer, you ask why again? Curiosity may be the single trait that differentiates the good salespeople from the great. We aren't there just to pitch a product; we are there to discover a reason why someone should do something different. The more reasons you can come up with, and the more you can justify them from a business perspective, the more likely you are to get someone to make a change. Curiosity makes this happen. When we are kids, we never stop asking why because we're trying to understand the world and how it really works.

Everything deserves a second and third level question. Great salespeople seek to understand. They don't stop asking questions until they truly understand all the problems; that's when they present real solutions.

A DAY IN THE LIFE – INSIDE, OUTSIDE, HUNTERS, FARMERS—OH MY...

A typical day in the life can vary depending on whether you are in inside or outside sales. As an inside salesperson, you spend your time literally inside your company's building - in front of your computer and on the phone. An outside salesperson spends most of their time in the "field": driving to meetings, knocking on doors, and being physically in front of prospects and clients. A typical week for an outside salesperson might mean being in the office on Mondays and Fridays in team meetings, setting appointments, preparing presentations, and doing other administrative tasks. The rest of the week is spent in the field, working your territory.

A territory, also known as a book of business, or book, consists of the clients or prospects that you're allowed to reach out to and work with. Once a company has more than a handful of salespeople, territories need to be created so that multiple people aren't going after the same company. Otherwise, salespeople fight over who gets credit for the deal, clients are confused, and the company looks bad. Most commonly, territories are defined by geographic boundaries, vertical/industry, or company size (typically based on a metric related to your solution, like company revenue or number of employees). The larger a sales team becomes, the more subdivided territories become.

Your main goal within your territory is to meet with as many people as possible, gather information, and solve their problems with your solutions. If you are not in client meetings, you will be prospecting to get more meetings (we will cover prospecting later, as it is key to your long-term success).

Client meetings are planned in advance and may take anywhere from 30 minutes to 2 hours. The size and complexity of your sales process will dictate how many meetings it takes to make a deal – it could be anywhere from one meeting for transactional products to over a year of meetings for high-level enterprise accounts. In lower-end, entry-level sales, a typical week could have you attending 15–20 appointments. As you become more tenured, you may only go on 3–5 appointments per week. A typical sales process involves a discovery call, a solution recommendation, and then a demo followed by a contractual process to lock down terms and conditions. Each of these steps might have to be repeated depending on the client's wishes, key decision makers' availabilities, and the scope of the project. For large deals, you can easily have 10+ meetings before closing a deal.

Next, let's talk about the two most common roles/categories salespeople fall in to: Hunters and Farmers. Hunter roles may be disguised by fancier terms like, "Account Executive" or "Business Development Representative," while Farmer roles could be called, "Relationship Manager" or "Account Manager." Most roles have a level of nuance requiring you to "Hunt" and "Farm: to varying degrees, but you still need to know what your primary focus of the role would be. This can likely be determined from the job description. It will usually be clear whether your primary goal is to find new clients or to service and upsell a current client base.

The role of a Hunter is quite clearly explained in the name: the job is to "hunt" for and bring on new clients. In general, it's harder to find a new client than it is to maintain a current client, so Hunters typically have higher earning potentials than Farmers. It takes a specific skill set to be a Hunter. As a person constantly seeking new business, you need to be a self-starter. This kind of job comes with a lot of rejection, and we mean a lot - like 95% of the time. You also need to be very good at overcoming objections and quickly proving your value to a prospect. People that have a high degree of success in these roles are

29

highly assertive; this gives them the natural drive to "argue" with someone. For instance, if you are assertive and your prospect says they don't want to meet with you, you will instinctively try to overcome that objection. It also helps to be impatient, as this will give you a natural drive to keep moving. This will help you develop a sense of urgency about scheduling the next meeting, adding to your pipeline, and moving your clients forward in the sales process. Hunters have a strong entrepreneurial spirit. They enjoy building something from nothing. They have trouble sitting still and always find a way to win. That is why many companies look for athletes, or folks with that competitive DNA, as they are used to putting in long hours in the pursuit of a goal.

Where Hunters are out trying to find new clients, Farmers are working hard to grow the current client base. Farmers are adept at building solid relationships based on trust. They are highly analytical people, constantly measuring and evaluating the performance of the product or service that the client has purchased. They will conduct regular performance reviews with their clients on a weekly, monthly, or quarterly basis. They are looking for ways to improve their customer's experience and help them maximize the value of their purchase.

Throughout these activities, Farmers are on the lookout for other solutions that a client hasn't yet purchased that may be a solid fit for their client. If a Farmer has done their job well, their recommendations are met with less resistance. The relationship, trust, and rapport they've established expedite the process.

This is an ideal role for an analytical person with a high degree of patience who is careful and strategic in their approach. It takes time to develop relationships with every stakeholder in the business, understand everyone's role, and know how your solution impacts each of them, but once you check those boxes, you'll know when and how to successfully present additional options.

As you are starting to see, sales is not a one-size-fits-all type of job. Based on your personality and skill set, there are multiple angles from which you could approach a career in sales. If you are a highly motivated driver with an entrepreneurial itch, a Hunter role might be better for you. If you like to play the long game, maximize a client's success, and increase the total value of the account for your company, a Farmer role may be better for you.

Something to be aware of, though: companies are always looking for skilled Hunters. Hunting is regarded as the harder of the two roles. So, if you have a natural inclination to Hunting, you'll often have more job offers and a faster career progression. By contrast, farming is playing the long game, which means you'll be in that role longer with slower career progression than your hunter counterparts.

Blended sales models, where a salesperson performs both functions, were once common. Though you'll still see a little bit of that today, more and more companies are moving to a specialist model - someone who is good at Hunting may not have the patience or relationship maintenance skills to be a Farmer, and a Farmer may not have the driving, entrepreneurial spirit to be successful as a

SECTION 1 RECAP

In this section, we covered what sales is, helped you understand the common myths of the profession, walked you through different types of sales roles, and discussed the key personality traits of salespeople.

Some key takeaways from this section:

1. ANYONE can do sales!

2. Sales is a viable long-term career

3. Sales professionals are not what they're made out to be

4. The best salespeople share some common personality traits

Yes, anyone can do sales, but think about how you naturally wake up and show up. Before we got in to sales, we were already extremely persistent, we hated to lose, we were both naturally curious about things, and we enjoyed solving problems. Sales helped us channel those traits, but the fact that they are a natural part of our approach enabled our success. It is well known that people grow faster in areas where they are already strong. Take this into account when considering a sales career. The more character traits you have that naturally that align with the traits of the best salespeople, the faster you will grow in the profession and the more energy you will wake up and end the day with. You can still be successful, but the more you operate outside of your comfort zone, the more your battery will drain and the more pressure and stress you will put on yourself.

Do you think you want a career in sales? If so, great, it's time to read on. We will give more advice on how to get your dream job and how to ensure success early on in your career!

SECTION 2 – GETTING YOUR DREAM JOB

Congratulations! You have decided to embark on a career in sales! You are in for a truly exciting life.

So, how are you going to get your first job? In this section we will discuss how to write a resumé, whether you have experience or not. We will help you think through things that are important to you, how to secure interviews with the right people, and how to manage the interview process and prepare the right questions to ask. We will sprinkle in some cautionary tales of the right and wrong ways to approach these things, and at the end, pull it all together with the best possible approach to secure just about any job.

UNDERSTAND YOUR LIMITATIONS & YOUR NON-NEGOTIABLES

When thinking about the jobs you'll apply for, it is important to understand your early career goals and what you are willing to do to achieve them. For instance, some of our best friends that we've known since middle school still live within 45 minutes of where they grew up. For the most part, outside of annual raises and maybe the odd promotion that comes along when someone retires or moves on, they've already maxed out their earning potential. Could they move to a major metropolitan area and instantly get a 20-30% jump in compensation? Almost certainly. Is that of any interest to them? No. They know what they want out of life and they're already getting it.

How quickly you can progress your career and what you're ultimately able to get out of it boils down to how hard you're willing to work and what you're willing to sacrifice. Are you comfortable working 60-hour weeks for years, living out of a suitcase five nights a week, changing companies when the next good thing comes along, moving across the country (or even the world), or learning a new language and adapting to a new culture for the right opportunity? You can make a lot of money, no question. Does that kind of lifestyle make it difficult to build and maintain any semblance of a social and family life? You bet it does.

Maybe you don't want to move out of your city because your family and friends are there, you never miss your Tuesday night basketball games, and you'd prefer not to have the headache of getting to know a new manager every few years. If so, you can certainly earn a good living, but you won't be maximizing your earning potential.

Which is the better path? That's 100% up to you to decide. There's no right or wrong answer here. There's no shame in having a modest pay check and a rich life outside of work and there's no inherent glory in earning $250k a year (although it can make life a lot easier).

When you're starting out or evaluating a new role, you need to understand your limitations, non-negotiables, and your goals and make sure they align with the change you're considering.

Take a few minutes to answer the questions below, then reflect on your answers – this exercise will guide your job search. It's OK if you don't know how to answer every question, but the more you can answer the better.

1. What would you like to accomplish in your career?

2. How much money do you need to earn?

3. How quickly do you want to get promoted throughout your career?

4. How often are you willing to travel?

5. Are you willing to relocate? If so, how many times and how often?

6. How do you define work/life balance?

THE RESUMÉ

Your resumé is a one to two-page sell-sheet that answers one simple question: should we interview this person? That's it.

It's best to think about your resumé and what employers are looking for in terms of key traits that fit a sales role. When companies are hiring entry-level employees, they're looking for culture fit and key personality traits that we covered previously. If you're fresh out of school and just entering the professional world, your resumé should include relevant coursework, extracurricular activities where you demonstrated leadership skills, and groups you were a part of that provide relevant stories to illustrate why you'd be a good fit for a sales job. If you're transitioning from a non-sales role to a sales role, you should hopefully be able to draw on other suitable leadership experience.

Key areas to include:

- Leadership Positions (clubs, sports, etc.)

- Goals or Objectives achieved (fundraising, organization growth)

- Projects you worked on, how you compared to your peers, and how you excelled

- Awards you received and how you won them

- Jobs you held, what you learned, and how you were willing and able to learn

- Community or volunteering experience

If you have experience, succinctly summarize what you did in each role and spend the rest of the space effectively professionally bragging. List your accomplishments as they relate to business achievements measured against goals and peers. Some key things you typically want to include on your resumé for each role:

- Your performance against quota— "125% to quota"

- Where you ranked on the team— "#1 out of 8 reps on the team"

- Average deal size and sales cycle length

- Average number of new meetings set per week, in comparison to your teammates

Recognize that because there's no standard resumé format, you can put whatever you want on it. If a particular metric doesn't paint you in a positive light, don't include it. Maybe you finished over 100% to plan but you were still only middle of the pack on your team. One stat makes you look great, the other makes you look average – use the better one

There are many free resumé template examples online.

The typical format would be as follows:

- Name—First and Last

- Contact Information—Cell Phone # & Email Address

  - If you don't have a professional email address, get one - they are free. The best practice here is some version of your name. As an example, firstname.lastname@gmail.com

  - (There's no need to include your address, it would only be used to screen you out.)

  - We have seen some very funny but ultimately unprofessional email addresses used: that's a major red flag.

- Objective—Everyone seems to have the same obvious objective- "to get a job with a company that allows me to grow/use my skillset/*yada yada yada*." So, don't bother with an objective statement – instead, focus on major accomplishments.

- Major Accomplishments—Hit them with your best stuff right way, letting them know what differentiates you and how you stand out.

- Education / Relevant Course Work—As you progress in your career the education section falls to the bottom, but since you are early in your career, this can be near the top. Don't forget to mention any relevant course work. For instance, did you take any professional selling classes, classes on business, etc?

- Career / Internship Information—Maybe you worked during college, had an internship, or worked full-time straight out of school. Here, you want to list the companies, how long you were there, any major successes and learnings, and overall highlight how that experience helped you get ready for the job you are applying to now. All experience is important: even if you were a cashier at a grocery store, you probably learned how to move quickly, be teachable, and interact with people in a positive way, and so on. Try to identify the skills, traits and experiences in your previous work that will tell your future employer more about you and what type of worker you will be for them.

- Awards—Most people bury this at the end. Instead, we suggest bringing it up to the beginning under, "Major Accomplishments." If you have won any less important awards that you didn't list under accomplishments, this is where you would put them.

- Lastly, any technical skills—here is where you mention if you speak multiple languages, or have any special certifications, or have experience with common programs like Excel, PowerPoint or Word. It is good to mention this, as that means the employer has less to teach you.

We live in the modern world - LinkedIn doubles as your digital resumé. Employers will still ask you for a paper copy, but you better believe they will check you out on LinkedIn and other social networking sites to see if the story matches up and how you brand yourself. Make sure you have sorted this out before you start applying for jobs. Here are a few things to make sure you have done:

- Use a professional headshot! If you need to pay a few dollars to get one done, it's well worth it. In a pinch, throw on a professional outfit, find a neutral backdrop, and ask a friend to snap some photos with a smart phone.

- Tailor the profile to sales. When describing what you did in school or work, tell a story that illustrates the core traits we've discussed earlier, especially if you haven't had a sales job.

- List projects, clubs, and other activities you did along with any outcomes that are relevant to a sales job.

- Remember, LinkedIn is for professionals, so design your profile with that in mind. Think of it this way: if it's on Facebook, it probably doesn't belong on LinkedIn.

On our website we've created a few resume templates that you can use for yourself. You can find them at http://www.salescareerguide.com

MANAGING THE JOB SEARCH

Take your job search seriously and put in the necessary time. The longer you go without a job, the harder it becomes to find the next one, and the faster you run out of money. Submitting 12 applications a day online and hoping someone reaches out to you does not constitute a job search. Think of the job search like a sales process: you are doing the research to prospect for opportunities, setting interviews, and moving the process forward with a goal of getting as many qualified opportunities (job offers) as possible.

This means you must plan. Put together a list of companies you want to work for, build contacts at those companies, network, and ask your contacts for advice on how to land the job. It also means preparing for interviews, following up afterwards, and eventually selecting the best opportunity.

The first step in your plan is to identify the companies you want to work for. When building your list of prospective companies, you must figure out what company's interest you. Here are some things to think about that will guide you in the right direction:

- Industries that interest you

- Products you are passionate about

- <u>Selling Power</u>, a publication that lists best companies to work for as a sales person

- Reputable companies where you know people

- Company reviews on websites like Glassdoor

- Searching the internet for "best companies in…" will bring you a lot of different lists to work from of as well

When thinking about these companies, it is important to consider how large and established they are. In small companies, you'll have the ability to affect the culture and make a large impact. You can often get promoted quickly in startups and small companies because you quickly become the most senior person there as they grow. There is also an inherent risk as the business models may shift rapidly and sometimes disappear altogether. They also don't have as many pre-defined processes and procedures. This can be good for self-starters and people who like to creatively figure things out. On the other hand, it can be very challenging if you aren't comfortable with a certain level of uncertainty.

With large companies, you are more of a cog in the machine and growth happens slower. However, you will likely receive great training, add an established brand to your resumé, and often get paid well since they can afford to pay more. There is also lower risk of getting laid off due to rapid changes.

There are clearly pros and cons to both but consider these issues as you build your list.

Here is an effective networking strategy you can use on LinkedIn:

- Identify people you want to network with. These will be people who currently or previously worked at companies you're interested in working for, in sales, sales leadership, or recruiting roles. When reaching out to people, make sure it's about them. People love to talk about themselves, their journey, and how they found success. The conversation will naturally come around to you but focus on them first.

  - Here is a template for your LinkedIn messages. Sales leaders— "Hi <first name>—I've been reading about <their company name> and I'm interested in<their industry> and the solutions you provide. At some point in my career I could see myself working for <company

name>. I would like to understand how you got to where you are and get advice from you on what I may need to do to work for XYZ."

- Salespeople— "Hi <first name>—I'm planning to apply to a sales role at <their company>. I see you've been there <approximately how long they've been there> so I'm hoping to learn about your experience there so far. Do you have a few minutes to share some insight with me?"

Recruiters— "Hi <first name>, I understand <company name> is a <leader/growing company> in the <their industry> space. I'm eager to learn more about the opportunities there. What's the best way for me to proceed as a candidate? The key in your messaging here is that it needs to be personalized. If you can effectively copy and paste the same message to different people at different companies, it's going to be painfully obvious to the recipient, and you won't be doing yourself any favors reaching out like that. Once you get the hang of it, it will only take you a minute or two to customize and personalize the messages to each person.

MANAGING THE INTERVIEW PROCESS

An interview process is like a wedding – if you've been to one you've been to them all – you know what to expect and how it's going to go, but each one is still unique. Every company reserves the right to interview in their own way. Expect 2–3 interviews in a well-managed process. For high-level roles, 5–7 interviews is not unheard of. And remember: the interview process isn't over until you have an offer letter in-hand or they've told you no.

Recruiting and interviewing is like dating with the intent of finding a long-term relationship. Both the candidates and companies are trying to solve the same problem from different perspectives. You want the best job you can get with your level of experience and the company wants the best available talent for a reasonable price. Seems straightforward, right? Well, yes and no. The company is trying to answer three questions when they evaluate potential candidates: 1) Do I like this person? 2) Can they do the job and do it better than anyone else that we're interviewing? 3) Can I afford them?

That's it. And in that order. If the hiring team doesn't like you, you're never going to get the job. No one is going to hire someone they don't like knowing they will have to deal with them for +40 hours a week— talk about a waking nightmare! After that, it's a question of ability. Based on your experience and how you behave in the interview process - does it seem like you can do the job? This is mostly a matter of your track record and experience. If your only sales experience is selling hotdogs in the stands of Yankee Stadium, you're probably not a serious contender for an enterprise software sales role (at least this time around). Finally, we're all budget-constrained, so if you're asking for 50% more than the other qualified candidates the company is interviewing, you'll have to be a bona fide a star in your field to command a compensation package that much higher than your competitors.

Let's walk through the process and the people you will be interacting with, and how these conversations typically play out. In this section we will also explain areas specific to negotiation. You will notice that this is a theme: whether you know it or not, and whether you're actively doing it or not, you *are* negotiating, directly or indirectly, through the entire process. Prior to getting an offer, you want to keep the conversation focused on job fit and alignment. Early on, you want to make sure the opportunity at least meets your minimum requirements. Beyond that, it's all about getting an offer.

Once you get to the stage of a verbal or written offer, the conversation shifts as you've gained negotiating leverage since they have selected you for the job. At this point, focus on questions that answer "What's in it for me?" It's all about getting the right offer and asking for everything you want that is reasonable. Remember, they are expecting you to negotiate because that is what salespeople do. It can be a red flag to not ask for more. As long as you ask in a reasonable way, the worst they can do is say no. It may be an uncomfortable experience for you if you're not used to advocating for yourself and negotiating, but understand that it is fully expected for salespeople to push for more. Sales leaders and recruiters know that in sales, you need to be comfortable asking the uncomfortable questions, and not leave money on the table or give things away to get deals. You must show that you are a business person and will protect their business when you are on their side of the table negotiating with a client.

The Usual Suspects

Here's a rundown of the motivations of the various characters who may be involved in the recruitment process.

Recruiter—A recruiter is typically the first official point of contact. Their job is to see if you pass the sniff test and if you align with what they are looking for. This will include your experience, motivation for joining the company, how you sound and carry yourself, whether you display drive, and of course, that your compensation requirements are within reason. Bear in mind that they are highly motivated to see you as a fit as they're usually incentivized to source qualified candidates and get them through the process as fast as possible.

It is also fair to ask them questions around what the manager is looking for. You can also ask their tips or advice for managing the next steps. Recruiters are also trying to protect their company, so they're not your friends, but they do want you to get the job since it reflects well on them.

Hiring Manager—Their motivation is to find the right person to help them achieve their goals, so they want you to win, too! But they are also cautious, as they have heard it all from candidates before. It's very rare for a candidate to say "No, I won't do that," or "that doesn't seem fair" or "I'm not right for this job." Inexperienced or desperate job hunters will say just about anything to get the job, so hiring managers are frequently skeptical. That's why using the STAR method (explained in detail on page 49) will be so important, as it focuses on real examples.

Hiring Manager's Manager/Other high-level executives—They are looking to see if you are consistent in the story you told the hiring manager. They will ask many of the same questions for this reason. They'll also be more experienced than the manager, meaning they're more sensitive to bullshit. They will focus a lot on you as a person and whether you can deliver on the expectations of the job. They won't care if you like them, or if you see yourself working well with them, as they are there to make sure the hiring manager doesn't make a bad hiring decision.

Peer/colleague/or other salespeople—They are looking for how you will fit in with the company culture, whether you are a good person who will work well on the team, or if there are any real red flags. They will be asking themselves if they'd enjoy working with you for +40 hours/week.

The typical steps in the process are listed in the following paragraphs. In each step, there is a chance to confirm expectations and do some degree of negotiating, not necessarily around money, but at least around expectations.

The initial phone conversation. This will take place with the recruiter. They will ask you about your background and level of interest in the job, as well as start setting expectations. The first step of negotiation takes place during this piece of the process:

Negotiation #1: Compensation expectations—Don't tell them what you are making—tell them what you want to earn. Guess what? If you say you're earning $25,000 a year, you will get an offer for $26,000 a year. If you tell them you are earning $25,000 a year and ask for $50,000, they will laugh at you and counter with a much lower offer. It's always about what you are targeting.

In-person interviews—This is the first of maybe 1–3 interviews where you meet your potential new manager. We will discuss this conversation, how to prepare for it, and what questions to ask later in the book. Again, be careful what data you share, it can and will be used against you in the offer process

Verbal offer – Negotiation #2. This is where you get a real number for the first time. It is the time to share any details, requests, or issues so the other person isn't hit by any surprises once you give them feedback on the written offer itself. You need to raise issues like whether you were expecting a particular figure and whether you can push for it, signing bonuses, relocation bonuses, and cell phone or car allowances. It's also the right time to say things like, "I've been thinking a lot about the job, and one of my concerns was the office hours or start times..." This allows you to check for flexibility if you really need it. For instance, you may need to drop a child off, or be home at a certain time, etc. Make sure you let these personal things be known before you get to the written offer.

Written offer – Negotiation #3This is your final chance to ask for things you want and to reiterate in writing anything that you spoke about informally that did not appear in the written offer. If it is not in writing, you can't count on it. When you are countering with a request for more money, you can use resources like Glassdoor.com or Salary.com to evaluate the offer and to research market rates for job titles at the company or similar companies. Glassdoor will tell you exactly what they have offered others, and what their competitors pay. Other online sources will give you an idea of overall market rates.

From David – I am currently mentoring a gentleman Kelly Pierce that is about to graduate college. He is going through the process of making a move from college to his first sales position. A few days ago, he says to me, "David, I have an offer, what do I do? They want me to make a decision in the few days." First, I let him know that they will pressure him to make a decision quickly to take him off the job market. I told him to let them know that he is very interested, he appreciates the offer, and that he needs about a week to give thoughtful consideration to the other companies he is interviewing with. This bought him time to think about the offer and to use it as leverage with other companies. He then went to all the companies he was interviewing with and said, "I have an offer in hand, but I am very interested in working with you - what are the next steps in our process?" This forced all of them to accelerate their processes, which in is now leading to multiple additional offers. This is where it's getting fun for *him. By the end of the week, he will have 3-4 offers to consider and then leverage against each other. Ultimately, he is looking at a combination of pay, sales training, and his level of excitement in the role. He can then say to each of them, "I have an offer where I am getting X more in base or sign on bonus" and politely negotiate, something like, "I am very excited about working with you, but I am considering all my options, and have an offer where the base is $10,000 more. Do we have any flexibility in the base we are discussing?" Best case, they say yes, worst case they say no, and most likely they will meet you in the middle. As a best practice, always say it's more than it is. For instance, if you are getting offered $5,000 more, say $10,000. That way, when they meet you in the middle you'll match the other offer or get even more in the best case. Now, don't be crazy, keep it in the ballpark and ask if it's possible - not a demand, but a request.*

Key takeaways here: your goal is to get multiple offers, 3 – 5 is ideal. You can typically delay the first one 1-2 weeks tops, but you need to be transparent as to why and keep the person that offered you the role in the loop as you progress. When you get all your offers, play them off each other. You are in sales - it's your job to negotiate and use leverage when you have it. But remember, it's never a demand, it's a "I am very excited, but need to balance my excitement for working with you with the financial implications. Is there flexibility? Here is what I am getting from others, can we figure this out? Can we meet in the middle? I don't want to be greedy." If you follow these steps, you will have options, and wherever you land will be the best opportunity with the highest possible financial reward.

Interviewing Techniques

There is a common form of interviewing called behavioral interviewing. The interviewer will ask open-ended questions about specific instances when the candidate was doing a task and how they accomplished it. The generally accepted best method of responding is known as STAR—Situation, Task, Action, and Result. If someone asks you about a time when you had to do XYZ, using the STAR method you'll respond by first explaining the Situation, and then the Task you had, the Action[s] you took, and the Result. Responding to interview questions with the STAR method ensures that you're clearly articulating your real experience. Prepare for this with specific examples of your background. Here is an example:

Interviewer— "Tell me about how you manage your prospecting outreach?"

"I am very methodical about prospecting. I see prospecting as a necessary activity when it comes to hitting my goal (Situation). Part of my prospecting methodology is large-scale monthly outreach (Task). I achieve this by making a list of 100 accounts and contacts on a monthly basis. I then create a template driven 8-touch email and direct mail campaign where I send a contact a handwritten note, and then follow up with emails until I get a meeting (Action). The outcome of this is I often get responses from 20% of the people I followed up with and half of those convert into meetings. This allows me to add roughly 10 new opportunities to the pipeline monthly, and with my close ratio at 30%, I close 3 of them. This has consistently enabled me to hit my goals (Result)."

You will notice how effective this type of question and response is. It tells the person you are interviewing that you have the experience, that you have a process, and that the actions you take clearly enable you to achieve the desired outcome you are looking for. Do your best to think of stories and scenarios in your life in this format, so you are ready to answer questions that come at you in this way.

If you get asked something and you don't have experience performing the activity in question, it is OK to be honest and say so. Redirect the conversation: "Can I provide you with a different example?" In this case, continue to use the STAR format, but maybe pick a time where you showed leadership ability or won an award, and walk the interviewer through the situation, task, action, and result you got from it. People will understand if you don't have experience in one area or another, especially when you're starting out. They want to know if you're willing to learn. Give them relevant details so they can picture how you may perform future tasks.

Before you interview with a company, should always do these things (once you have some practice, you can knock this out in less than 20 minutes):

- Read the company website—look at their Product Offering, News Reports, Annual Report, About Us, their career site and anything they say about the job and their culture.

- Read Glassdoor reviews - but take them with a grain of salt. Regular, happy employees don't take the time out of their day to post reviews, so if they skew a little negative, don't worry about it. If there's a trend of negative reviews with the same topics popping up, keep that in the back of your mind.

- Look up anyone you expect to meet, and the members the sales team, on LinkedIn and take notes on their profiles.

- If you don't already know their industry, identify their top competitors – this is as easy as googling "<company name> competitors") and how they compare on key metrics like employee count, revenue, company age.

- If it's an in-person interview, look it up and drive there at least a day in advance so you know exactly where the office is, how long it takes to get there, if it will take extra time to find parking and walk in. Aim to be at their door/in the lobby 5-10 minutes before your interview starts. Much more than that and it's strange, much less than that and your interviewer might become concerned about your ability to plan and execute basics tasks.

Model Answers

Here are some questions you need to be prepared for along with some ideas of what a good response and a bad response look like:

Question: "What do you know about our company?"

Bad Response: "You guys make 'this widget' or 'nothing'" or "Not really sure, I think you do this right?"

Good Response: "At a high level, tour business is <X size> in revenue, with <Y number> of employees. You seem to specialize in these <main product/service offerings>. What excites me about those things is <ABC>. When I looked at your competitors, I felt that you do <ABC better than them."

Question: "Why do you want to work here?"

Bad Responses: "I need a job" or "Your company looks cool" or "You are the only company that called me back."

Good Response: "I have done my homework, and I have chosen to apply for this job. The reason why is that I am very passionate about <their product/service offering>. I believe that I can get behind what you do and help potential clients get excited about doing business with us in the future."

Question: "Tell me about your prospecting strategy?"

Bad Response: "What's prospecting? You know, I'll call people? I don't have a strategy, I figured you would teach me? Huh?"

Good Response: "I always believe in a methodical approach to things. The first thing I would do is grid out my territory by types of companies. Then, I would figure out which were the largest or best fit companies in my territory based on the criteria I am sure you could provide to me. From there, I would pick the companies I want to reach out to and find the right contacts on LinkedIn, their website, news, and other ways and places. Then I will work with my sales leader on the best possible messaging to send to these companies. I would then deploy a multi-touch marketing campaign, where I would call, email, use social outreach, and send them direct mailers for handwritten notes on why they should meet with me. Based on my research, it requires 8+ touches to get someone to respond, so I am prepared to design strategies with my leader to accomplish this in a variety of ways." (Then pause and wait for their head to explode—you may get hired on the spot with this answer.)

Question: "Tell me about a deal you won and how you won it."

Bad Response: "I haven't won any deals."

If applicable, remind the interviewer that this is your first sales job, and offer to tell them a story about something you accomplished.

Good Response: Remember the STAR format! "I haven't won any deals, but, let me tell you about a personal success I am proud of."

From David: As an example, pick a real story that will bring out real emotion in the interviewer. It doesn't need to be as heavy as this, but this is the best example I have, outside of professional experience."

Key point here—I know nothing about home building! So, when Hurricane Harvey hit Houston, my house flooded. It wasn't as bad as some, but we got about 8 inches of water in our house. The water was in and out of our house in about 2 days. You can imagine our devastation. (SITUATION) Now, my biggest goal was to get my house stripped down as fast as possible so I could dry everything out and start rebuilding. (TASK) My first step was to rip out all our carpets which took all of day 1: my wife and I alone did this. It was a very tough day. The next day, we got lucky as a group of volunteers started assembling in my neighborhood: that day, 10 people removed all the dry wall in my house on the first floor, including all the wet insulation. The next day, my co-workers came over, and we removed all the hard wood floors, baseboards, door trim. The next day, we started disinfecting beams and using enough fans to turn my house into a wind tunnel. We bought a bunch of dehumidifiers, and within about 2 weeks, we got our house to a point where it was ready to be rebuilt. During that time, I sourced contractors. Because I was willing to pay cash, I was able to get them to do my work before others who were waiting on insurance. I made a list of all the tasks that needed to be done, gridded out a calendar of when each step needed to happen, and project managed each contractor on their step and timeline. Things didn't go perfectly... I have a story about Lowe's customer service that would make your head explode, but I had luckily found good people who showed up on time, got paid, and moved on. There is a lot more to this story, but those were the actions I took. (ACTION) The result was that I had my house rebuilt in about six weeks. It took money, time, pain, and many sleepless nights on my part. While others were sleeping, I was painting. While people were going home, I was researching next steps, best practices, costs, buying home materials and so on... I put everything I had into this, day and night, probably 18+ hours a day. I had neighbors who took 3 months, 6 months, and some even a full year to put their homes back together, but we did it in a fraction of the time. (RESULT)

Again, I am not a project manager, nor am I a homebuilder. But I consider this one of the biggest nonprofessional wins in my life. My family was faced with major disaster, and we recovered in the right way, the fastest of anyone I know. Like we do in sales all the time, I was able to stare adversity in the face, make a plan, execute on the plan, and never let emotion, fear, or the "I can't do this" feelings get in my way. I am a doer and I made this happen. This is how winners behave, and this is what your interviewer wants to know: If we hire you, how will you do everything in your power to win!?

Question: "Tell me about a deal you lost and why and what you learned?"

Bad Responses: "I don't lose deals" or "Nothing comes to mind."

Good Response: If you have a professional story, share it. If not, again, think about something you didn't win at, and what the takeaway was. Always think of using the STAR format. But what the interviewer is looking for is not so much the negativity of the loss, but the sense that you reflect honestly and grow from your failures.

For instance— "I recently lost a deal with XYZ company. What I found out at the end of the process was that they picked my competitor because someone I didn't know was the main buyer who actually made the decision, and the person I was meeting with was a gatekeeper/influencer, not a real buyer. What I learned from this is to get much more specific in my questions about their ability to sign the contract, who else would my solution impact, who my competitors are, who they have met with, the pros and cons the client sees in the potential options, and so on. This change in my process will help me with that kind of deal next time."

Question: "How do you like to be managed?"

Bad Responses: "I hate being micromanaged" or "I don't need to be managed."

Good Response: "I like it when there are clear expectations. If I am struggling or not hitting the expectation, I'd want coaching on how I can improve. I see the manager/employee relationship as a partnership where you are helping me understand what I need to do, I will go out there and do it to the best of my ability, and then we can work together on ways to continually get better at those tasks.

Question: "Tell me about a boss you worked for and what you didn't like?"

Bad response: Any negative stories! Keep it professional. You can't say, "Oh, this guy was a *$(#, he did this to me once…" Look, we all have those stories, keep them to your friends and family.

Good response: "I believe most people have the best of intentions, but sometimes personalities just aren't a good fit. I've had experiences where people have been passive-aggressive, or not told me ways I could improve when they should have at the time. I like being coached, and I like learning and growing. What I would ideally like in a leader is open and honest communication."

Question: "Why do you think you would be a good fit?"

Bad Response: "Because I am awesome!"

Good Response: "You know, based on our conversation, it seems like you are looking for someone to do <XYZ> that has <ABC traits>. If I were to compare what I believe you are looking for, to me as the potential candidate, I see overlap in all the areas. I want this job, I am excited about what you do, and I believe I will be very successful at it. I also know that I will have a lot to learn, and I look forward to learning from you and the team. I have been successful at just about everything I have put my mind to, and I will do what it takes to be successful here and help us both hit our goals."

Bonus Tip! The folks we have been most impressed with build a presentation that showcases what they know about our respective businesses, and how their skills and passions align with that business and why we should hire them. It doesn't need to be long, just 4–5 slides. At the start of the interview they have said, "You know, I have done some research up to this point, can I share something with you?" And they have opened a tablet or laptop and literally pitched why we should hire them. It is also a great way to gain control of the interview and demonstrate your desire to join the company.

It is important to remember that for many entry-level jobs, hiring managers are looking for cultural fit. This means they'll be searching for qualities and traits like: self-starter, intrinsically motivated, passionate, coachable, and curious. They want to find out if you can work well on their team. Do you hold yourself accountable, or are you likely to blame others? How do you present yourself? How do you respond to questions? Are you argumentative, overly agreeable, or thoughtful and articulate? All these things (and more) can be determined by your responses to their questions. If you are new to interviewing, it may be helpful to practice with someone who will challenge you and ask you tough questions. This might be a parent or a friend who has been through this process before.

It is also of the utmost importance to have a list of questions prepared for your interviewer. Remember, an interview goes both ways: just as they're looking to see if you are a good fit, you are also trying to see if you will like working there. You're asking yourself whether you can make this company a home for a number of years. The questions below will help you learn a lot about the role and whether you see yourself being happy there. These kinds of question also convey to the company that you've done your homework. This is attractive to the company and may suggest you're a good fit because it demonstrates that you know what they're about and want to be there for the long haul.

Questions to ask while interviewing

- Why is the role open?

  - Is it because the team is growing, or because they need to replace someone?

  - If growth, understand why. If it is a replacement, find out why the previous person left or failed. This will tell you a lot about the leader and expectations of the job, as well as what they will be looking for in the next candidate. No one wants to repeat the same mistake twice.

- How long have you been with the company? Why did you join? How has your experience been?

- How big is the team you're considering mc for and how long have the team members been with the company? Companies with long tenures in their leaders and salespeople often have good cultures and incentive plans.

- Tell me about your background.

- What sales management experience do you have

- What are the expectations of the job?

- How many people are on the team and how many hit quota last month/quarter/year? How many were above quota?

- What are your best people doing differently than your lower performers?

- What are your top priorities? How would I help you achieve them?

- How long has each person on the team been with the company?

- What are their professional backgrounds?

- Can I meet one of them?

- How much and what types of travel I can expect?

- What does a typical week look like for someone in this role?

- What does the onboarding and training program look like?

- (As the interview is wrapping up)—Do you have any hesitations about my ability to perform well in this role?

- **Lastly, always end the meeting by asking for next steps in the process—remember, you are interviewing to be a salesperson and this is what sales people do. This is expected.**

After the interview, wait a day then send a thank you email to the people that you interviewed with.

These should be customized, individual emails. If for some reason you don't have enough information to customize the email for each person, send one email to the group. Otherwise they'll compare notes and see you sent the same generic email to each one, which won't bode well for you. In this email you should note a few things that you liked about the conversation you had with them that stood out to you. The follow-up should be short, thanking them for their time, reiterating why you would be a good fit, and stating how excited you are about moving forward in the process.

Just like when you are dating, you don't want to seem over-eager or desperate, but you do want to show that you care, that you want to move forward, and why you would be a good match. Also, remember that you are applying to be a client-facing salesperson. Anything you do during the interview process will be seen both through the eyes of the person you are speaking to *and* perceived through the lens of how you would act with a client. So how you follow up will be an example of how you will treat a client. People that don't follow up quickly and thoughtfully always fall below people that do.

Here is a sample thank you note. Remember, tailor this to each person if possible and make it your own:

Hi [first name],

I enjoyed our conversation yesterday and appreciate the time you took to see if your sales opening would be a mutually beneficial partnership. I understand that:

- You are looking for someone who excels in XYZ, and I will.

- You are looking for someone that has [traits] and I do.

- You needed someone that was passionate about selling ABC solution.

With all that said, I want to move forward. I want to join your company and help you hit your goals. Based on our conversation, I hope you agree that I am the right candidate and that you can see me positively impacting your business. If you have any concerns, please let me know and I will be happy to discuss those with you.

Thank you again for your time and the opportunity to learn more about the role here. I am excited about moving forward.

Thanks,

<your name>

Follow up with the recruiter and hiring manager you met with weekly on the status of the application. It would be fair to include anything new or relevant that you believe will catch their attention and remind them why you would be a good hire. Do this until you get the job, are told the position has been filled, that you are no longer being considered, or to please wait and that you will be informed about next steps when there's an update available. There is a balance between being persistent in your follow up and flat out frustrating to deal with, though. If you're new to sales following up as frequently as we recommend will likely be outside of your comfort zone, but less so than is actually annoying or would hurt your chances. Again, this would be mirroring how you would act as one of their salespeople, and we all know that following up to get a sale and demonstrating why someone should buy from you is key to our profession.

PUTTING IT ALL TOGETHER

To reinforce the ideas in this section, read this story from Scott Barker, one of the movers and shakers at Sales Hacker and Outreach. He approached getting his dream job in the same way he would approach landing a big deal. This is an example of the best possible way to proceed. What we have written above should be the standard and we don't recommend you do anything less. However, what Scott did raises the bar. If you follow his practices, you're almost guaranteed to get the job you're looking for. *Quick shout-out to our friend Scott Ingram, host of Sales Success Stories podcast, and Scott Barker for sharing this story with us and allowing us to publish it in our book.*

From Scott Barker - Beating out the competition to land a sales job is hard. Beating out 300 applicants for your dream job can seem nearly impossible. However, every amazing experience that I've had thus far in my career has been somewhere on the other side of "impossible". In this story, I'm going to share with you how I was able to cross the seemingly impossible chasm and land my dream job:

I loved my job. I was 24 years old, a business development manager at a fast-growth SaaS (Software as a Service) startup, had hired a team full of close friends & we were all crushing it. I really had no intention of going anywhere but sometimes opportunities are put in front of you that are too good to let pass you by. A company that I had been following for a long time, Sales Hacker, was looking for a new head of partnerships & I immediately knew I had to throw my hat in the ring. The network I would gain would act as a springboard for my career. So, I got tunnel vision and went to work.

The problem? 300 other sales professionals were also gunning for this job and many of them worked at Tier 1 tech companies like Salesforce, DocuSign, or Adobe, had way more experience, and had gone to fancy business schools like Duke, Stanford or Columbia. So how did I manage to tumble out the other side of the hiring process?

Here is my step by step process for landing any sales job:

1. **Always Be Connecting**: The work starts before you ever even find your "dream job". You have to be constantly networking as a sales professional so that you're in the know about upcoming openings. Make sure that your LinkedIn profile is crisp at all times. You never know who could be looking! In my particular case, the only announcement was a LinkedIn post so if I wasn't part of the CEO's network I never would have even known about this opportunity.

2. **Follow a Process**: Reframe your mind to start looking at the hiring process as you would your sales process. In my case, I even told the hiring manager from the get go that I was going to do my best to go through this process as I would with one of their partners. If you're not rock solid on this process, which is arguably the most important sales process you'll ever run with them, then how can they expect you to rock it with their clients? In order to apply you had to complete a Google form with eight questions. I made sure that I had thoughtful answers & bugged a friend to proofread for me. Attention to details & speed of responsiveness matter—don't shoot yourself in the foot before you begin!

3. **Engage Multiple Stakeholders**: Now it's time to engage other stakeholders and find yourself a champion! I reached out to the person currently in the role & another person in the C-suite. Try to set up a

zoom call (video on), lead with curiosity and position it as you wanting to make sure that it's a perfect fit for both parties. This is the perfect time to showcase that you're a good culture fit that and that you're someone they'd want to work with every day. I was able to make a strong connection with the VP of Marketing who would act as my champion throughout (shout out Gaetano DiNardi).

4. **Take an Omni-channel Approach**: I made sure that the hiring manager (in this case it was the CEO, Max Altschuler) knew who I was—I went all in on email, LinkedIn, Twitter, and Instagram. Think you're being too pushy? I'll tell you right now, you're not. Maybe if you were going for an engineering role but this is sales: persistence is good.

4. **Be Passionate & Prepared**: After all that, I was given the opportunity to jump on a phone interview. I was pretty nervous so I tried to focus on the things I could control. In this case, I knew that even if I wasn't the smoothest, I could certainly be the most passionate and prepared. I came to the interview with an agenda, I knew their (TAM) Total Addressable Market I had a 30-60-90 day plan, I knew their offering through and through, had some suggestions/tweaks they could possibly make, had a list of answers (or stories) for common questions and of course had some intelligent questions of my own prepared. Make sure you always get concrete next steps!

5. **Send a Video Follow-up**: As soon as the interview wraps up, make sure that you're following up, thanking them for their time & reiterating how excited you are about the opportunity. In my case, I sent a quick video instead of just a normal email to try to further separate myself from the pack.

6. **Stay Busy**: Now, at this point, most people play the waiting game. But you have to ask yourself, just like a sales process, is there anything that I could be doing that would increase my chances of getting to the next round? For me, it was staying active on their social channels with

thoughtful comments and looping in with my champion to do a quick debrief on the interview.

7. **Always Get Next Steps**: Now for the real interview: I was on to the next round, which was your classic longer, more formal video interview. At this point, I started to let myself hope that there was a chance, so I doubled down & made sure I had my best success stories down pat. At this point, my main goal was to explain exactly how I'd get us to where we need to be while showing how passionate I was about the organization. You need to show that you're not just looking for a job, you're looking for THIS job. Of course, try to close next steps and ask if there is anything, they can see that would stop you from getting the job.

8. **Go Above & Beyond**: I'm overly critical of myself so I left this interview thinking that I didn't hit on a number of points that I had hoped to bring up. Luckily, I was told the next day that I made the shortlist: It was me and one other person. I don't think I slept for two days … but once again, I asked myself "is there anything I could do right now to improve my chances?" I decided there was! So, I ended up hiring a graphic designer to help me build a sales deck on "why I was perfect for the job," I even included quotes from all of my past bosses in there.

9. **Do A Hiring Review** (like a deal review): I got a phone call the next day from the CEO saying that it had been a ridiculously difficult decision, but I GOT THE JOB! He even let me know that he was leaning towards the other guy who had a lot more experience. Apparently, it came down to the video I made (which he had watched with his girlfriend which put her on my side), the fact that I had an internal champion and the fact that I went above & beyond with the sales deck.

10. **Focus on the 1%**: Needless to say, I was pretty excited & looking back, it wasn't one thing that I did but the accumulation of everything

that turned the tide for me. Everything I did got me 1% closer to my goal and that's exactly how you should be looking at your sales process.

Little did I know the work was just getting started but after a lot of late nights, it led to the best career year of my life & I was able to close 1M dollars in revenue in my first 9 months on the job. Well above expectations!

And to top it all off, one of the partners that I signed, Outreach.io, ended up acquiring our company less than a year later and now truly the sky is the limit!

I hope this inspires you to go out there, put everything on the line and land your dream job!

A CAUTIONARY TALE

From David - Fresh out of college, I was facing the dilemma of what to do with my life: I could either go to graduate school and delay starting my career or get a job. Since I was broke, and my parents stopped giving me money, I decided to go into sales professionally. I interviewed at multiple companies and, not knowing a better way to make my decision, chose to work for the one that paid the most. I didn't really take anything else about the company into account.

Four months later, I found myself sitting in my college fraternity house, 22 years old, and I'd just quit my first "real professional" job. It was paying more money than I thought possible to do something I wanted to do for the rest of my life.

I was scared. I felt like I made a crazy mistake and I had no idea what to do next.

Before I go further and discuss how I moved on to my next job—and ultimately a truly fulfilling career in sales—let's go back four months.

The job was with a large robotics company selling solutions to automate factories. My territory was the state of New York. The regional office of the company I worked for was in Ramsey, New Jersey—roughly 400 miles away from Rochester NY, where I was living. The company I worked for had a rule that seemed to make a lot of sense at the time; their sales reps had to be in the office Mondays and Fridays to set up meetings for the following week. This meant I was commuting 400 miles to work on Sunday, 400 miles home Monday night, running a territory the size of New York State Tuesday—Thursday, and then commuting back Thursday night to the office and 400 miles home again on Friday. And while I could have stayed in New Jersey over the weekend to minimize my travel, I also wanted to have a life, and my life was back in Rochester.

This was during the winter. If you have never lived in that part of the country during the winter, I'll tell you this—snow, ice, and overall weather conditions are not conducive to that amount of weekly travel. But I was doing it weekly. Sometimes I would drive, sometimes I would fly. The easiest airport for me to fly into was John F Kennedy, more fondly known as JFK, which to me stood for, Just F@#$ing Kill me. I slept in that airport more times than I could count. By the way, I hate flying.

As if all this wasn't enough to burn anyone out, this company also had no formal training. At the time, I knew nothing about time and territory management, so I was all over the place. If anyone spoke to me, I would meet them in person, whenever they wanted, wherever they were. This made for some really long days and nights. Suffice it to say, I had made a huge career mistake. For the better or worse, I have almost no patience. I looked this situation squarely in the eye and said, "I'm done."

As we have said before, it's not all about money. If you are chasing the money, you need to ask yourself what you're truly willing to do to get it and what will happen if your initial expectations don't pan out? There are other hugely important aspects of any given job, like sales training, company culture, who your boss is, and what the expectations of the job really are. Not all companies and jobs are created equal.

So, what happened after I quit?

Thank God for Google. I had committed to sales as a career path. I loved it—the freedom, the money, the power to influence and ability to impact a business like no other position. I was still hooked on that idea. But I had realized that I was an untrained newbie, and I knew I needed to do something about that. So, I searched the internet for "companies with the best sales training." Fortunately, a publication called "Selling Power" came up. It was a GOLDMINE. It listed the companies that had the best sales training and paid the best.

So, what would any entrepreneurial salesperson do? I applied to all of them ... all 50 companies.

ARAMARK called me back, and I went on to spend 4 years there. They have some of the best sales training in the world. One of the first things they taught me was time and territory management—how to grid out a territory to be in certain areas on certain days and when to say, "No," to travel. If only I had known that a few months earlier!

I learned in a very short time how much I DIDN'T know about sales. They taught me various methodologies and styles like appreciative inquiry, closing skills, how to prospect, how to manage a pipeline, and much more. They gave me a solid foundation from which I could grow. I have learned a lot more since then, but the decision to join a company with solid sales training set me on the path to sales success.

Looking back on this part of my life, it's glaringly obvious that I had a lot to learn. I'm grateful, though, that I had the courage to recognize I was going down a path that would limit my long-term growth. It may seem like an obvious choice now, but it was a very difficult one then. I try to live by the philosophy of failing fast, learning from it, and not making the same mistake again. This may mean I take more risks than others, but it has also put me on a faster path to success. The desire to not repeat past mistakes is what led me to find a company with good training and to realize the importance of building a strong foundation with a company that really knew what they were doing when it comes to sales.

SECTION 2 RECAP

In this section we walked you through exactly how to get your first sales job!

Some key takeaways:

1. This is your future - the first few companies you work for will be the foundation of your career. Pick the right ones, do your homework, and make smart decisions for the right reasons. If you chase the money, but are miserable, you won't be your best self and you will end up back where you started in no time.

2. You can't conduct a good job search by applying to one or two jobs a day. A proper job search is a full-time job in and of itself, treat it accordingly.

3. Career sites and online application processes are a black hole. Can they work? Yes, but you also need to be networking and reaching out directly to hiring managers and potential future colleagues to get your foot in the door.

4. Interviewing is like dating - it needs to be a good fit on both sides. How you handle the process, questions you ask, and the follow up you have will make the difference between getting a second date or getting ghosted.

Please follow these practices. If you don't, you may not get the job you want, or in the worst case, no job at all. Your first job is your foundation. Like he shared, David made a misstep in his first job, but it wasn't a big one, and he didn't let it last long. He stayed in his second job for four years, and it taught him a ton. Being willing to fail fast, learn from it, and move on is one of the reasons he excelled so fast in his career, and what set him up for future success. He has learned a lot along the way, but being willing to leave his first job quickly, and join a company that would teach him the fundamentals required to ensure he was doing the right things in the right way made a huge difference. Make your choice wisely. Follow the advice above and you will be off to a great company at the start of a winning career!

SECTION 3 - WHAT DO TO IN YOUR FIRST YEAR ON THE JOB

You did it! You landed the job! We are proud of you! Now, as a wise man once said: "Don't be dumb."

Seriously, don't mess this up. It's easier than you may think, and this may be a brand-new world for you. The rules, the expectations - everything is serious, and it needs to be taken that way. In this section, we will help you to avoid all the common traps and make sure you get off to a good start. You will learn best practices for your first few weeks including how to treat people, how to align yourself with the right characters, and how to accelerate your learning. We will teach you how to build early pipeline, remove roadblocks, and manage your days and weeks. Towards the end, we will help you to understand how to manage the political landscape you may or may not realize you have just been thrust into, as well as how to find mentors to guide you along the path.

Buckle up - your life just got a whole lot more interesting!

STARTING THE JOB

Remember - getting the job was the first hurdle. Now, you need to follow through on everything you said you would do. If you don't, your integrity will be in question and you will make the leader that signed off on you look bad. Think of it like this: you just joined the varsity football team. You need to show up to practices, be a good team member, and execute the strategy of the coach. You need to block, tackle, and help your team win games. If you can't handle the basics, you will quickly get cut from the line-up.

The best way to do this is to stay pumped and stay humble. Here are some quick ways to make a good first impression.

Meet with your boss and do the following:

- Discuss a 90-day plan and talk about expectations on a weekly basis.

    o Take a lot of notes and confirm exactly what you will be doing and when.

    o When you are new, you're allowed to ask questions about anything and everything. Confirm key pieces of knowledge and ensure you understand tasks you are given. If you don't confirm them on the spot, you will frustrate your superiors and damage their trust in you. Businesses expect you to professionally raise your hand immediately if you don't understand something or need help. Every second you waste will impact on the time needed to complete the task, and time is money. The caveat is that somethings you can and should have the self-sufficiency to figure out, and you don't need to bring every little thing to your manager's attention. If you don't understand something and you can't figure it out after looking at the first Google search results, then bring it up.

- o Find out who in the office has the most tenure and success. Ask your boss for their endorsement to shadow that person.

    - Best practice is to offer coffee or lunch to pick their brain because you understand they're very good at what they do. It's literally as simple as that.

From Andy - I once did something similar in a medium-sized organization I worked for after I'd been there a few months. Having been there a while, I'd identified the movers and shakers in the company and wanted to see what I could learn from them. While I tried to insist that I pay for lunches, literally no one let me as they were senior, and I was clearly a rookie rep. After a few of these meetings, I started getting informal and formal offers to come work for their teams—not my intent by any means, but it goes to show this isn't purely a self-serving move. People deeply appreciate being asked for their advice.

- o Take notes on what you do every week, who you spoke to, what you learned, what tasks you completed, and what you need help on. If you run into issues, document them for discussion. At the end of each week, sit down with your leader and review this list. Not only will they be impressed, you'll also show them they made a good hire that's ramping up, getting things done, and hungry to learn more.

- Ask your manager these questions:

  o What are my KPIs (Key Performance Indicators)?

    ▪ Begin with the end in mind – understanding how you'll be measured gives you perspective on what's most important to your success.

  o What are *your* KPIs?

    Understanding how your manager is being measured helps you understand how best to work for him or her.

  o Knowing what you know now, how would you go about starting off in this role to ensure success if you were in my shoes?

    ▪ Be careful with this one, it's smart to also bring your own proposed solution to the table while asking this, otherwise it might look like you're just asking your manager to do your work for you.

  o Who on the team is the best at prospecting?

    ▪

  o Walk me through the week of a top performer.

  o Walk me through a typical sales process from start to finish.

  o Can you give me a list of the people I will interact with frequently?

    ▪ This should be one of your first tasks, meet all those people, learn what they do, and how to best work with them

- Are there any books or podcasts, etc. you recommend that could help accelerate my progress?

- Frequently ask them how they would handle situations. When you are super new to it's acceptable to simply ask. As you gain experience, you will want to have a suggested plan and then ask for their feedback on your plan. Otherwise it can come across as lazy. You can never go wrong by doing what your manager suggests. It may not always work, but if it doesn't, you can point back to the fact that you did what they suggested.

From David - To give you a real-world example, let's go back to my time at ARAMARK. It was an experience that laid a great foundation for my career. I was hired at ARAMARK by the GM, and when I was hired, I did this exact thing with this GM. I built a plan and met with him weekly. This allowed me to get to know him and build a solid relationship. I worked at his location for three years and I never stopped doing this. Of course, over time, our conversations evolved from discussions of expectations and weekly tasks to developing personal rapport and eventually to celebrating the deals we closed. I was promoted three times in those three years. The GM always knew what I was doing, what I was focused on, and if I was achieving my goals. It also gave him great insight into me as a person. If I ever needed help, he was there. At the end of each of those Friday meetings, I would shake his hand and say, "Thank you." I truly was thankful for the job and the trust had in me. When my wife wanted to move to Houston, he endorsed it and convinced ARAMARK to pay for the transfer. On my last day at his branch, we shook hands and reflected on the relationship we had built. He told me how much he'd miss me coming into his office, talking about my week, and shaking his hand to say, "Thank you." This 30-minute meeting turned into one of the best parts of both of our weeks, and I look back on my time with ARAMARK and that GM fondly.

Much of your career, especially the early stages, can be supported by the above actions. However, those things alone won't cut it. You will need to create quick wins. This is often easily accomplished by doing everything asked of you. If you take the corporate training seriously, get clear expectations from your boss, and mirror the top people in your office, you will see success. Figure out what the best people are doing then get out there and do it consistently. It isn't luck - it's all about activity and skill. You learn the skills as you get the experience.

There is a hugely popular sales book called *The Challenger Sale*—if you haven't read it yet, it's absolutely required reading. One of the areas it studies is the behaviors of successful salespeople. To save you some time, they boiled it down to two main personality types that were most successful: Hard Workers and Challengers. Hard Workers won most in low complexity sales (likely your early career jobs), whereas Challengers won most in high complexity sales. The behavior of Hard Workers is easy to replicate: simply outwork everyone around you. If the benchmark is 100 calls a week, make 200. If the goal is 10 meetings a week, set 20. It's simple: work harder, do more, get more sales. When you're starting out, you don't necessarily have all the skills and knowledge of a tenured sales professional. If you simply outwork everyone around you, you will be successful early in the game.

By contrast, Challengers are defined as people who *teach*, *tailor*, and *take control* of a sales process. This requires product knowledge, business acumen, confidence, and tact. These are learnable skills that will be pivotal as you develop into a true sales professional. However, this book is not about sales process, becoming the best salesperson out there, or all the processes you could follow to do that. It's simply to ensure you get off to a good start and build the foundation for a successful career. With that said, early in your career, your focus should be just to work harder than everyone around you. It really will give you more opportunities to learn and practice skills.

One further thing to note: once you have left college, you have left college. Don't go out every night. Get your rest and be a business professional. Take your new life seriously - your future self will appreciate it. When you progress faster, earn more, and see more success than your peers, it will all be worth it.

THE EVOLUTION OF SALES

From Andy - Last year, I closed the single largest deal of my career. From the first time this Fortune 100 client responded to our prospecting efforts to the day when the contract was signed, it took six months. There were three separate demo meetings—the first had one contact, the second had three, and the last had at least seven, including the Chief Human Resources Officer. Along the way, there were multiple internal strategy meetings, calls with my main contact who championed me through this process, and some really "fun" and interesting contracting calls with legal teams after we received the verbal "yes, we want to buy" from the client. If that sounds like a lot of work, it was - but it was well worth it. Here's the thing though—that was only the part of the sales process that I witnessed. Before our second meeting with them, the client was searching for and conducting back-channel reference checks on us, reaching out via networking groups to find our other clients to get an unbiased viewpoint. They wanted to know the answer to questions like whether we're easy to work with, whether our platform and service live up to our claims, and so on. This kind of thing happens all the time—buyers are smart to do it, and arguably too trusting if they don't.

Think about a decision you recently made. Maybe you were in a new town trying to decide which restaurants were worth checking out, or maybe you were considering buying a new electronic gadget. You probably checked Yelp for restaurant ratings and referred to Google for customer reviews. Before even going into the store, you already knew the pros and cons, the average price, and all your wish list items. Maybe you didn't even leave your house and got same-day shipping from Amazon.

We may be showing our age here, but this process and concept didn't exist when we were growing up. Even when we were in college, this process was in its infancy. Now that we have seen full adoption of this kind of buyer behavior, the world of professional selling has changed as well.

It is well-known in the modern sales community that buyers are more educated than they have ever been. This change in buyer behavior demands a modernized approach to align with modern buyers.

When your buyer knows your product and your competitor's product as well as you do, how do you sell? In some instances, if they are well connected, they may have more knowledge on real use-cases than you do, since they have people in their network who have used both your product and your competitor's product. Any stories you try to tell in a presentations won't carry as much weight as the real-world stories their network tells them about your solution and service. As such, here are a few things a salesperson must be able to do very well:

- Be a business person first— Strong business acumen is required. This is the ability to get people to understand the value of the change as it relates to their business processes. You must truly understand and be able to communicate the business implications of your solution, both financially and strategically.

- Really KNOW your product - the good, the bad, and the ugly. Understand what it says on your website vs. how it really works. Your buyer has done the research and knows what solutions are available, so you must truly know the ins and outs of your solution. The best way to get this knowledge is to speak with your company's implementation & operations teams. What common difficulties are clients facing during installation? Speak to your customer service team – what are people most often complaining about? Speak to your customer success team—what do clients love about the solution? Try to understand why your customers stay, and why they leave. These conversations will give you insider information that may not be publicly available. You will have the ability to respond to the narrative with real data and better maneuver your common objections.

- Competitive Intelligence— You should never bash your competition, but you do need to help your client understand the differences between competing products and how those differences may impact business objectives. Position yourself as a consultative business partner. Remember, your buyers are informed, so you must go deeper than the online information and marketing narratives - seek out the tribal knowledge of the industry. As a new salesperson, this can be tough - seek out the senior salespeople to help you.

- Listen WAY more than you pitch—In the past, you could pitch hard and pitch often – the salespeople with the best pitch alone could win. This may still be the case in some situations but remember: buyers have read the marketing materials and watched the online demos. This means a strong discovery (A discovery session is a conversation where you ask many questions on the current state of someone's business, their desired future state, and discussing how those changes could positively impact their business) is required, which requires discovery sessions that last two to three times longer than your pitch. Seek to truly understand every aspect of your client's operations and processes that would be impacted by your solution. Find out where they've been, where they are, and where they're going. Ask questions to figure out the problem they're facing and bring it to the surface. This allows you to build a strong business case for change before even presenting a solution.

- Working in a multiple buyer environment— Solutions are getting more complex. Every company is building products that solve multiple problems. This makes their solutions stickier (i.e. more likely to increase your chances of holding onto a client because changing from one solution to another is too much of a pain) and increases their share of customer spend. This also means there are likely multiple buyers involved the process. If you are not directly seeing them, they will be behind the scenes. Your product will touch multiple lives within a company, and it's your job to touch as many of those people as you can. Those are your buyers, influencers, and champions. The practice of "consensus selling" is very important to the modern salesperson. Many salespeople will meet with one person, think they've built a relationship, and falsely believe they've secured a deal. Meanwhile, the competition consulted with the four other people behind the scenes that would be impacted by the solution. Who has a better chance of winning: your one great relationship, or your competitor's five?

The rise of public information has changed the game for every industry. To succeed in the modern era, you must be educated, know your solution, know the research your prospects are doing, establish connections with multiple buyers, and always strive to be an excellent businessperson.

WORDS OF WISDOM

We asked hundreds of salespeople "Knowing what you know now, what would you tell your younger self when you were first starting out?" Pay close attention to these tips: these people have been in your shoes and know the challenges to come. Following these principles will save you time, allow you to learn things faster, and ultimately be more successful. If you are seeking wisdom, here are words from the wise:

- No fear—Just do it
- Fail fast & learn
- Listen more, to everyone

There's a ton of value in these three mantras, so let's unpack each one in-depth:

No fear—Just do it

We have managed and mentored many young professionals in our careers. Almost all of them feel like they need to know all the scripts, know all the presentations, and need all the information before picking up the phone. This is avoidance at best and fear at worst. There is a reason Nike adopted this as their motto. The message is this: don't talk about running, go run; don't talk about losing weight, eat better.

Being hesitant to take action is hands-down the most common challenge new sales people struggle with. You are in sales - you are the Navy Seals of the business world. You can't let fear hold you back! Face that fear head-on and *just go do it.*

In the beginning, all you need to be good at is picking up the phone or knocking on a door to ask for a meeting. Then you can figure out what you need to do from there, which is usually to ask a lot of questions. When you first start you actually need to know very little about your products and services. You just need to be great at setting appointments. Your company will prepare you to handle product discussions. Once you start meeting with buyers your product knowledge will grow quickly. They will ask you the questions they need answers to, and even though you might not know at first, you'll be developing a study guide that tells you what you need to know.

This may seem to contradict what we have said about the knowledge levels of the modern buyer. Yes—you will need to know a lot and will need to learn it quickly. But don't let that slow you down. As long as you are sitting there, too afraid to pick up the phone before you know everything, your competitors are talking to your prospects and locking down your contracts. If that doesn't scare you more than picking up the phone, you may be in the wrong profession. Remember - it's OK to fail here and there, but it's never OK to not act. Everyone in your company knows that you're new. They accept that you'll need some time to learn the ropes.

Fail Fast & Learn

Action breeds failure and failure drives knowledge. Learn quickly by taking action and failing fast. Get out there, set meetings, talk to people, listen, ask questions, and if you don't know something, write it down, figure it out, and get back to people quickly.

Remember—you are new to this profession. There will be far fewer negative repercussions from your mistakes than when you are in high-level enterprise accounts. Failure on a $5,000 deal is much less serious than failing on a $50,000 deal.

From David - When I think about early failure, I go back to my job at ARAMARK. This was many, many years ago, but this scenario still sticks out to me. I was a junior salesperson and my Vice President of Sales was in town. As the young upstart that I was, I lined up some meetings - one of them was to close a deal. Now, this is where the beauty of young arrogance comes in to play. I went right up to my VP of Sales and said: "Do you want to come with me to close a deal?" He looked at me, but in a way that made it clear he was looking right through me. It was arrogant of me to think that this guy who runs a division with over 100 salespeople in it would want to come with me to close a small deal. That request was wrong, but I didn't know any better. I wanted to make a good impression on the big boss. I wanted to climb the ladder quickly, and thought "What better way than to close a deal with him?" You know what he said to me? He said, "David, I love nothing more than closing deals. Tell me, why do you think this one will close?" Great question! My answer: "This guy loves me ... and he said he wanted to do business with me." I remember this, because he just started smirking and said, "Oh really? Have you asked him if he is ready to sign today?" My response, as my tongue hit the floor, was "Um ... no." His response, "OK, go ask that, see what he says?" He already knew what the outcome would be because he had been there and heard that exact thing, probably 10,000 times from salespeople like me. So, I went and asked. The response was "NO. I am not ready to sign today, I am evaluating multiple vendors."

Let's pause here, as this to me was a massive process failure that my VP taught me in an almost perfect fashion. A client liking you and a client saying they may even want to buy your solution is not a client saying they will buy from you. From that point on, I NEVER forecast a deal until I had built a

83

timetable around when it would close. This is as simple as saying "It looks like this may be a good fit / It looks like we can really solve a problem, do you agree?" "Yes." "Great, are you ready to move forward?" "Yes.", "Great, let's talk about next steps." Then you move to the implementation timeline phase of the process and work backwards from the client's desired go live date, then you move into dates contracts need to be signed by to hit those outcomes and get the client to agree to those timelines. You can adapt this to your own requirements, but that is the general idea. Once this is accomplished you can now hold yourself and them accountable to hitting the required milestones, including when contracts need to be signed to hit all the required dates.

Now, I've had so many more failures that I could write a book on failing. The point is, don't be afraid of it. Ask the tough questions of yourself and your clients. Run your opportunities past your boss and more senior people. You don't know the blind spots yet, so let them point them out to you. The best people fail often and LEARN from their failure. Learning is the critical part.

From Andy - During my second full year in sales I closed the biggest deal of my career to date. It was a fantastic feeling. At the time I was an agency recruiter (or headhunter) within Houston's Oil and Gas market. I'd found and brought on a new client, met with them, understood the needs of the organization, put several qualified candidates in front of them, and secured a good offer for my candidate that met his requirements, so he accepted it. It felt great. I was about to bring an additional $38,000 to my firm. (For context, an average deal for our team was around $15,000.) I was *already thinking about how much commission that would turn into and what I'd be spending it on. About a week later my client sent me one of those emails that makes your blood run cold, something like "Andy, call me, we need to talk." Very long story short, my candidate ended up going radio silent during the typical pre-onboarding process, and my client wanted me to figure out what was going on. I reached out to the candidate. Instead of answering my call or calling me back, he emailed me to set up a time to talk days later— not good. I already knew what was happening. So, we finally got on the phone Friday and I asked him what was happening. He used a lot of words to tell me that he'd decided to stay with his current company instead of joining my client's company. It hit me like a ton of bricks. My revenue, my commission check, my pride. Eventually some less self-centered thoughts came to me: What about my team and office who were counting on that revenue to hit our goal? What about my client that needed that key hire? I was in a funk. I didn't get anything done the rest of the day. That night, I'm not too ashamed to admit that I drank my sorrows away and blamed the world for my troubles.*

A few days later when I finally let my pity party end, I spent some time thinking back through that entire sales process and my pride finally let me admit that I'd been sloppy—I'd skipped small but important points in my rush and excitement to close a deal. Now, there's no way of knowing if I'd run a better process my candidate still wouldn't have backed out— trying to figure that out is impossible and a waste of time. And besides, it's not the important thing here. The important thing here is that if I'd done everything I could have done, as well as I could have done it, and the deal had still fallen apart, there would have been no reason to be upset (at least not in the "drink your sorrows away" way.) It's natural to feel bad when something you've worked hard on blows up in your face. The value is in learning what went wrong, how it went wrong, and specifically what you can do to not make the same mistake again. It's an easy thing to read and nod along to, it's a very different thing to learn through your own failures. These days, years later, when a deal doesn't go my way, I let management know, we do a debrief, figure out how to adjust our strategy moving forward, and that's that. No emotional funk, no "I don't know how to deal with my stress" pity party binge drinking, just next steps and action.

Listen More

Have you ever been in a conversation where you can see the person waiting to respond, like a cat ready to pounce on a mouse? We've seen this on the face of more junior salespeople that we can count. stop. Seek to really understand.

This isn't just about listening to your clients. It's about listening to your company, your boss, your peers, your clients, and yourself.

Let's break those down a little bit.

Your company and your boss

Toss your ego out of the window fast. You do not know better than them, you are not special, you are new to a company. Your company has probably successfully trained and nurtured hundreds, if not thousands, of people before you. Your boss was probably one of those successful salespeople, if not at your company, maybe at a competitor. Whatever they tell you to do, do it, without hesitation—then if it doesn't work, bring that back and debrief with them. But to start with, just do what you are asked to do. You have not earned the right to re-invent or change the game. Try it their way, adapt it to your style only once you have mastered it their way. Then, you can recommend changes slowly as you gain traction if they are needed. But again, if for some reason changes really should be made, you are challenging years and millions of dollars in training that have been invested in teaching you, the new person, how to do your job. This is still partially true even when you enter a new organization with experience. You just haven't earned the right yet. If you need to ask your new boss one question, once you have confirmed what they want you to do, it should be, "When do you want it done?"—Now that question will *really* get you ahead.

Your peers

Your peers are the best people to ask if you have questions about your solution, your competition, and other up-to-date field knowledge. Be careful about going to them about things your boss or company has told you to do. They are there to fill in real world knowledge gaps. If you don't default to what the company says you should do to start with, you put yourself at a lot of risk. If you do what the company told you to do and it fails, you are safe. If you don't listen to your boss and you do listen to a peer, well … you both just got fired.

Your peers are the best when it comes to asking things like, "What questions do you most often get from prospects? What are the real bestselling features / functionality? What objections do we get most often, and how do we overcome them?" They will know in real time better than your company. What prospecting strategies are working for you? Align yourself with the best salespeople in the office and learn all that information from them. It's easy; buy them lunch and build the relationship until they trust you to go on their calls.

Your clients

Becoming an expert at listening will make your paycheck get bigger, doubly so when you're client-facing. Do not listen to respond, listen to understand. Peel the onion. Onions have layers and so can lines of questioning. Don't settle for a first-layer response to a question. Follow up your questions with probes like: "Explain that better," "Tell me more," "How does that impact your business?", "How does that impact you personally / professionally?" Asking these follow up questions is how you'll learn the important things that allow you to win the deal. One of the greatest failures of new salespeople is when they accept the answer to the question and move on. For example, say you ask, "How do you like XYZ product from our competitor?" (the product you are trying to displace). The client often has two responses, and they are some variation of "I like it," or "I don't like it." Most junior salespeople will just say OK, and then move to the next question. But let's really peel the onion on this question:

- You— "Do you like XYZ solution?"

- Prospect— "Yes, they do a great job." (The harder of the two answers: "I hate them" is always easier).

- You— "I am happy to hear that, what do you like about them?"

- Prospect— "They have great service and the solution meets my needs."

- You— "Great, tell me about how they have handled service issues in the past."

- Prospect— "Well, this went wrong, and this is how they handled it."

- You— "Glad they handled it well. What other service issues have they handled for you?"

- Prospect— "Well this time, and this time, and this time ..."

- You— (DON'T MOVE TO SOLUTION YET) "Glad they are on their game when things arise, any other service issues that you have had? "Always get to the final answer on a line of questioning. Then you can move on to talking to them about service hours, and dedicated vs. shared service and so on:

- You— "What do you like about their product?"

- Prospect— "It does XYZ for me really well."

- You— "Glad you are happy. Does their solution do this, this and this?"

- Prospect— "Yes, it does two of those, it doesn't do the third."

- You— "Well, what happens when the third needs to happen?"

- Prospect—<response>.

- You—<clarify response and ask about other things that you know are differentiators.>

- Prospect— "Huh…"

- You— "I am glad you are happy, but when you mentioned service, here is where our service is better, when you mention product features, ours has XYZ. With that said, if you were to make a change, would there be any value for you?"

- Prospect— "Maybe, let me ask you..."

You are about to get asked a ton of questions on your solution: answer them, but steer the conversation back to the change, the value of the change, and the business implications (both good and bad) of that change. At this point, the conversation has shifted to change management: stay there, gain the commitment to explore the change - it is the most important thing.

We could keep going, but the point is for you to know how to peel the onion on even simple question like "Are you happy?" This is the process for every question of relevance. Ask those 2nd, 3rd, and 4th

(etc.) level questions until you really understand what a client means by their answer to the question. People will often try to hide things because they don't know or trust you yet. Their initial answers are usually guarded and geared to giving you as a little as possible while keeping the conversation moving, as a lull in the conversation is awkward for everyone. Keep the ball in the air but move it down the field while digging in to all the answers. These details will give you the ammunition you need to sell the solution. Without the right answers, you are selling the wrong solution. The number one sales technique you need to get good at is asking questions and listening. You aren't really responding to anything. It's simple, just ask them to tell you more about what they just said and keep steering the conversation towards those areas where you want to learn more.

You can take the same approach with your boss and your peers. People will make assumptions that you know more than you do – they'll give you the benefit of the doubt. Because of this, they may tell you as little as possible to convey the message because they don't want to waste time. It doesn't do you any good to pretend you understand. If you don't fully understand, or you see value in what they are saying but you want to know more, dig deeper.

From David – I get called on frequently to test out new products from vendors that sell solutions for sales people. A vendor approached me from a lead generation company. I typically don't take these calls because the company I work for has a very clear evaluation process for these types of solutions - they don't let people just try them. They go through budget committees, enterprise-wide feasibility processes, integration processes, etc. But they had a decent pitch and the sales guy said that their CEO wanted my feedback on their solution. I figured that was BS, but it piqued my interest and appealed to my ego. During that initial call, I was very transparent with the sales person. I didn't have budget and I don't make decisions, but if something impresses me, I will ask the right people if they would be open to evaluating it. I explained this, and the sales guy even acted a bit put off, like I was wasting his time. But I was upfront and honest about it and he chose to have the call anyways. After the call, I told him that I liked a few areas of their solution and I would ask my sales operations partners if they would be open looking at it. I went and did that, and the feedback I got was that they had multiple priorities, and that they were looking at solutions for this, but they didn't want to engage right now. I took this feedback to the salesperson at the AI vendor. I explained what I did, our process, and that now wasn't the right time, to which he responded, "You are our contact in our CRM tool, so we will continue to work with you," which was a very bizarre response. I ignored it. A few weeks later he followed up with me and asked if I am ready to move forward. I ignored that as well. Then a month passed, and we were approaching the end of the year, and he reached out to tell me his CEO was changing their business model, and if I wanted the same pricing, I needed to buy now. I ignored that too, then he followed up after the New Year, with a one last offer that he begged to get me a favor on, to buy now.

The missteps here are amazing. I do not normally ignore people, but his follow up was so off the mark I was either going to ignore it or give him a piece of my mind. He obviously wasn't listening and didn't seem to be coachable, so I figured I'd take a slightly higher road, and not just repeat myself - so I hoped he would go away. Again, to the point, he wasn't listening at all. If he was, he would have taken a way different approach. I clearly liked what they had, or I wouldn't have gone to my sales operations team to get their thoughts. But instead of taking my feedback and understanding the fact that I couldn't buy even if I wanted to, he pushed me hard. I would have been an internal coach for him, I would have reviewed his account strategy plan and helped him with it, heck, I would have told others about their solution. Now I am a detractor, and I even felt compelled to put this in the book. Please, truly listen to your clients. Don't hear what you want to hear, listen for what they are really saying. Not everyone will buy your product, but if you listen to them and approach the right way, most people will listen to you... unless you're a jerk.

Yourself

Lastly, listen to yourself. This is your life, no one else's. You need to live with yourself and you need to be your best self. If something is wrong, talk to your boss about it. If things aren't working, be upfront. If you run into setbacks, ask for help. Be honest with yourself on your growth and progression. Always seek to get better and learn from mistakes. Part of this is doing a strong debrief after every major interaction and asking yourself: "How could I have made that better?" or, "Where did I make mistakes?"

From David: I mentioned earlier that one of the best decisions I ever made was leaving my first company after only a few months because I was not getting the training and leadership I needed. That was a hard decision, but it was one of the best I ever made. I listened to myself when I felt it wasn't working. If you are going to fail, fail fast, be decisive, and move on.

GOALS

Simon Sinek is an amazing motivational writer and speaker. One of his most successful books was *Start with Why*. If you haven't listened to his TED Talk on that subject, stop reading now and go listen to it. It will help you understand your driving motivations, which will help you craft your goals.

Can you be successful without setting goals? Well, you might find success in the short term without goals, but staying motivated and consistently delivering results every day, week, month, quarter, and year will be a serious challenge and you will burn out. That is why figuring out your own motivators is so important. They will help you to wake up feeling excited about achieving them.

Share these goals with your boss, your significant other, and your friends. They need to know what your goals and motivations are. This will help them help you stay on course. Here are some important questions you need to ask yourself now, and every few years as your life changes:

- What am I willing to sacrifice to achieve my goals?

- How much risk am I comfortable with?

- What is the plan to achieve the goal?

- Do I have everything I need today to achieve the goal, or do I need other tools or to learn new skills?

- Is it a SMART goal (Specific, Measurable, Attainable, Relevant, Time-bound)?

Personal Non-Business

If you are new to goal setting you may not know what a "working backwards plan" is. It's simple. Say you want to lose 15 pounds and you have 13 weeks to accomplish it. What do you need to do each week to make that happen? Each week you need to take a couple hundred calories per day out of your diet. This is where the plan comes in. Each day look at how are you eating. You'll find that you're asking yourself: "Is that the right snack? Do I need another slice of pizza? Do I need to have a beer right now? Maybe instead of soda I should drink water for 90 days."

Personal Business

The same sort of process can be used in business. It may look something like this: I need to sell $1 million this year, my business says I need to have a pipeline of $4 million since we have a 25% close ratio, so I know we will lose 75% of those deals. I know my average deal size is $100,000, which equates to 40 opportunities that I need to get into at an average of $100,000 to build the necessary pipeline. That's about 1 new opportunity per week, right? Wrong! There are sales cycles in play too, so if your average deal takes six months to close, and you are one day into the year. You need a $4 Million pipeline by six months into the year, which means you need to set about 2 new appointments a week, remember, you don't have 52 selling weeks. You have closer to 40–45, with client vacations, your vacations, and corporate training days—and it's always good to be conservative too. So, to get into 40 new opportunities, I need to set up about two meetings a week. To set up about two meetings a week, I know that I need to reach out to 25 people to get one meeting, which means I need to reach out to 50 people every week. But wait, there is more here, not everyone that accepts a meeting will become an opportunity. Let's assume that 50% of the people you meet with, agree to a sales process with you, which now means you need four meetings a week, and 100 calls.

Let's recap the math quickly as it will be helpful to understand this. While these numbers are arbitrary, this is the type of planning you should do at the start of every quarter and year to ensure you have your goals properly mapped out and that you are on track to hit them. At any point in time, you can always recalibrate based on real time data and achievement of those goals.

- What % of people decide to work with us once they meet us?

- 100 calls a week = 4 meetings (this is your outreach to accepted meeting rate).

- 50% fall out, so that equals 2 qualified opportunities.

- $200,000 a week has been added to the pipeline.

- Across 6 months, adding a consistent $200,000 a week = a $4.8M pipeline

- You can expect another 25% of those to fall out by the end which should leave you with $1.2M in closed dollars

- Congratulations—you hit your goal!

You will notice something very important here: the deals that you prospected week 1 close week 26, deals you started week 26 close week 52, and everything in between. This is how you create consistency in sales - through constant top of the funnel pipeline building. Sales isn't perfectly linear like this, but it isn't far off. Imagine you took two weeks or a month off from prospecting? You just missed your goal OR went a few weeks without selling something in the future. Consistency is king … so stay consistent!

Client Focused Goals

Let's look at one more form of goal setting, which is based around helping your clients to achieve their goals. This is known as the calendar close, and it is one of the most effective ways to get a client to move forward once they have selected your solution. It's an important goal setting skill as it ensures your clients hit their goals through your solution. The calendar close starts with asking your client an important question: "When do you want a new solution like mine to be live?" They might say they want it in 4 months.

Now you can say "Great, let's talk about what needs to happen between now and then." You work backwards: "It takes us about a month to implement our solution, so we have three months left. It takes us about a month to draft contracts and negotiate legal language based on experience, so we actually have two months to get to that point. So, if you want to be live in four months, we only have two months to get through the steps it will take to make your decision. Who needs to be involved and how do we create a project timeline with you and those people to make sure we hit those timelines? What are the steps in your buying process that we need to account for? Let's put those milestones on the calendar and work together towards achieving them."

This is a more advanced skill, but it is something you should learn and get good at as fast as possible. There is nothing worse than getting to the end of the sales process, and having client say, "We are ready to move forward with you and we want to be live next week." If at this point, you must explain it will take a month to negotiate the contract and a month to go live. It will cause all sorts of problems. This approach sets the right expectations, creates urgency on both sides, and aligns you and your prospect on a plan to help both of you hit your goals.

BUILDING YOUR BRAND

"A brand for a company is like a reputation for a person. You earn reputation by trying to do hard things well."

- Jeff Bezos

When "building your brand" is discussed in a business, it's a question of what people think about you when you are not around. This is an important thing when it comes to individuals, as well. Your brand is the sum of your reputation, the decisions you've made up to now, what you value, what you do, how you look, what you say, and how you say it. Companies have a brand, but so do you. Your brand is for you to choose and control. By demonstrating key behaviors, you have ownership of how people perceive you. For instance:

- Are you a hard worker?

- Do you seek to bring people up or down?

- Are you always seeking to make things better?

- Do you complain or solve problems?

- How often do you listen to your superiors and do you do what they say?

- Do you get things done and find creative ways to do so?

All of these are examples of brand builders or detractors. There are many more.

> *From David - I am known in my business as the guy to go to when you want to solve complex problems. If it's a tough task, give it to David. I am also known as a disruptor and a challenger, someone who is not afraid to give people bad news or force change where needed. According to my Stand-Out profile, which is a personality assessment tool my company uses, I am an Influencer/Advisor, which means I approach situations trying to get people to see my point of view and advise them on a course of action. This can sometimes be seen by others as telling them what to do, which can be good or bad depending on who I am speaking to. This sometimes forces me to explain my personality to people who don't know me well and adapt to where I am coming from. The point is, every interaction that you have with someone in your business will impact and form your brand. Do everything you can to make sure interactions, even challenging ones, end positively.*

Seek to understand other people's point of view. If you'll indulge us getting a little esoteric and philosophical, from a game theory perspective, everything we can be categorized into one of two types of "games" that we all play: finite games and infinite games.

Finite games have clearly defined rules and ends. They have points which determine winners, and losers. Think of sports, board games, even a semester at school. You can consider a single prospecting call as a finite game, or an entire sales process as a finite game.

Infinite games have no clearly defined rules and no clear end. Many people approach their careers as a finite game – it's a very easy trap to fall into. People seek to "win" in all interactions. "Winning" or "getting your way" can become more important than how people felt or if you're even creating any real, long-term value. It's like when the used car salesman crushes your hand in a way-too-strong handshake. Sure, some people consider that a "dominant move" and he may have "won" the handshake, but is it really helping anything other than his own ego? Are you more or less likely to engage with him on any meaningful level after an experience like that? Please understand that focusing on the finite games, the short-term wins is important, but not to the exclusion of all else. Don't hurt your ability to win the long-term wins, the infinite game, by focusing only on what's immediately in front of you. How you made someone feel is more important than any other outcome. People will forget most of the outcomes - they will always remember how you made them feel.

From Andy - Years ago when I worked at the international recruitment firm Michael Page, I had many, many layers of management between myself and the CEO, as things go in multi-billion-dollar companies. As it happens, one of our board members, Patrick, was very interested in the business unit I was a part of. Being a busy person himself, he didn't reach out to us directly (he was in Sao Paulo, Brazil, while I was in Houston, TX), so instead, he had his intern, Doug, reach out to us. Doug was (and is) a great guy, but at that time Doug hadn't yet graduated university whereas I had years ago and had been successful in sales and in this business for quite some time. You'd think that when Doug called I might miss it, or if he emailed something over I'd get to it when I got to it, or maybe even wait for him to politely follow up before I deigned it worthy of my time and attention—after all, I was making the company money, Doug was just an intern, right? Wrong. Dead wrong, actually.

We had a nickname for Doug in our office: the most powerful intern in the world. Was that entirely factually accurate? Maybe not. Did it have a lot of truth to it? Yep. Here's the thing, Doug wasn't just Doug, some random intern. Doug was Doug, Patrick's right-hand man. So, when Doug asked for something, it was Patrick asking. And if Patrick asked for something, Patrick got that something, and he got that something very quickly. If Patrick asked you to jump, you didn't ask how high, you just started jumping as best you could while gathering feedback on your jumps to see if they were to his liking.

The point of this story is that titles don't mean much and often, the people with the most influence in an organization aren't the ones you think. Humans are funny, tribal creatures. We generally like the people we spend time with and we generally value the opinions of people we like, even if they're not otherwise qualified to make those judgements. So what? All the more reason to be polite and respectful to everyone you interact with. Especially when you're new to someone, they're trying to make a judgement call—are you worth their time or not? People are constantly looking for reasons to screen new people out, so if you give the wrong person a bad impression, your deal (or your candidacy for the job) is toast. On the flip side, if your prospect is having a tough time deciding between you and a competitor, it's often the little things that make the biggest difference—like how the receptionist mentioned the thank you card you sent to her for helping you get your laptop set up for a presentation. Scott Barker's story that you've already ready at the end of Section 2 "Putting It All Together" is a perfect example of this.

WHAT HAVE YOU DONE FOR US LATELY?

Now that you understand what sales is and isn't, you should also have a fairly good idea of your potential role and a day in the life. Let's dive in to what you are accountable for. In sales, you are always measured by your most recent sale or set of actions. The previous month or year quickly falls by the wayside, so keeping up with the key measures of performance is critical.

Metrics

The first major aspect of performance to consider, and arguably the most important leading indicator of future success, is metrics. All sales reps are judged by some set of metrics, also known as Key Performance Indicators (KPIs). The most commonly measured metrics are pipeline generation, meetings weekly, total value of your opportunities, revenue generated, and the number of new clients you bring to the business annually. All of these are key indicators of current or future success – we'll unpack each of these below.

Revenue

Revenue is the universal yardstick in sales. It's the end result of all the hard work. Revenue appears most often in the form of closed business related to a goal. Depending on your role, you may have weekly, monthly, quarterly, or annual goals. How you rank compared to your peers or the business benchmarks is ultimately how you determine if you are being successful in your role. This is one of the nice things about sales: right, wrong, or indifferent, you always know where you stand. This is one of the things that sets sales apart. In many other roles, you may have an idea of how good you are or what people think of your work, but often, you need to wait for a performance review or for someone to directly give you feedback. In sales, you know in real time how well you are doing. This can be very comforting or downright scary at times. You need to be comfortable in your skin and accept the fact that everyone knows the good and bad sides of your performance. If you feel like this is something you couldn't handle, know it is a big part of being in sales.

Pipeline Generation

Above all other metrics, this is the strongest determination of future success. You will often hear the term, "peaks and valleys." That's because when the pipeline is strong, people often stop prospecting because they are "too busy." For the love of all things, don't take this approach. Always be prospecting. The people who block time every week to build the pipeline are the ones who do 200% or more of their quota. They simply don't let the valley happen to them. Especially early in your career, if you don't have sales coming in, the ability to hunt is one of the strongest, most desirable traits an employer is looking for.

of Meetings set and attended

The other key metric is how many client facing meetings you have weekly. In theory, if you are any good at sales, the more meetings you have, the more deals you can progress forward, and the more sales you will make. That's why this is such a closely watched metric.

Total Value of Opportunities / Your Pipeline

Most of the time, your key objective is to close business, and since business typically doesn't close in a day, you have a pipeline. The pipeline is made up of all the prospecting work you have done. Most companies look at the value of the pipeline, and based on the business close ratio, they determine the health of the pipeline. For instance, say you need to close $100,000 in sales every quarter and on average, the business closes one in every four deals they go after. That means you have a 25% close ratio. In that scenario, a healthy pipeline would be $400,000. Because, as we know, no one in sales closes every deal they chase, so to hit your goals, you always need to have a pipeline way above the target.

BUILDING A PIPELINE

Prospecting is the best way to show success before deals close and to demonstrate to your new employer that they hired the right person. As we advised earlier – find out who the best prospector on your team is, spend time with them, and emulate what they do.

To give you a basic foundation to prospecting, here are best practices when getting a new territory:

1. Get a list and sort it by the largest companies - the bigger the company, the more money they are likely to have, and the larger your deal will likely be.

2. Break that list out by vertical categories—Healthcare, Engineering, IT etc. Ask your peers and your boss what your most successful verticals are, and where you have the most successful case studies. Take the top 10-20% of this group. That should narrow down your list to the best fit opportunities. Bear in mind that most salespeople can't manage more than 100 accounts at a time.

3. Once you have the best fit list, find contacts. There are typical buyers of every solution, whether it be HR, IT, Operations, Marketing, etc. Ask your boss, "Who in the business do we typically sell to?"

   a. Now go to LinkedIn, visit company websites, and look for the highest-level person that typically buys your solution.

4. From there, start putting together messaging. Once again, ask your boss for the best case-studies for each vertical and the

best messaging your business has used to gain access. He or she should have it or know where to get it.

5. Put together a cadence, or series of sales activities. This is often an eight-touch campaign (this is where you will reach out to someone eight times in a variety of ways over a defined time period, typically 6-10 weeks). Write 4–5 emails, a phone script, a voicemail script, and a social message that is much shorter. Plan a handwritten note with a case study and a small gift to include as a touch. Put them in a scheduled order and then execute. A common cadence is to start with 1–3 emails, followed by a social touch, phone call/voicemail, few more emails, and then a direct mail package.

6. Eight touches are the average it takes to get a response, sometimes it will take less, sometimes more, but eight is a good average to work from. You have done your homework, you know they are a good fit, and you know you've have had success in their industry. The point here is, stay persistent.

A good tactic that's very effective if you spend a lot of time physically driving around your territory: get a map of your territory and split it up by geographic area and day of the week. For instance, on Monday you're on the north side of town, Tuesday you're downtown, Wednesday you're on the southside, Thursday you cover the outskirts, and Friday you're in the office. When you are setting appointments, it will help you with time and territory management since you can say to a prospect, "I am in your area on Thursdays," and you can run your prospecting activities based on those days as well. This really helps you maximize your days. Imagine if you didn't do this and you had 3 appointments in a day, all 10–20 miles apart - you just spent half your day driving around whereas if all three were within one mile, you would have had hours back in your day to knock on doors, drop off business cards, or pop in on people to try and get more meetings.

One highly effective method of in-person prospecting is called T-Calls.: When you are meeting with a client company, visit both their neighbors and go across the street to form a T around your first meeting. Essentially, when you are meeting with someone, canvas that area and look for other companies that you may want to meet with as well. Walk around business parks, go inside every door, collect business cards and drop off marketing materials. On the following day all those business cards you just collected are now your prospecting list for that day. Call and say, "Hi—I stopped by yesterday and left you my card and some material, I was meeting with XYZ company in the area and they really saw value in what we have. Can we set a time next (fay you are in the quadrant) @ 2pm for us to meet for 30 minutes to discuss ABC?" Keep doing that and build your days around it. You just became VERY efficient with your time and everyone in an area now has your information so when you follow up, it is easy for them to reference you. Now you aren't cold calling, you are following up since you literally were in their office the day before. That is a much warmer introduction.

Consistent prospecting is one of the most important ways to be successful sales. Everyone will tell you they work hard and that they prospect. The people who really focus on prospecting show significantly better results than their peers.

SALES PROCESS

Sales is the process of identifying potential customers, or prospects, and guiding them through the buyer's journey (or sales funnel), which consists of the following steps: awareness, interest, consideration, intent, evaluation, and finally, the promised land of BUYING. Depending on your company, some of these steps may be handled by your marketing or advertising team, but these are all fundamentally sales activities.

While the customer facing interactions are hugely important, they are only one piece of a successful sales process and, in general, only represent a fraction what a salesperson spends their time on. There are many different types of sales processes. The most important thing here is that you build and develop your own sales process.

From David – The sales process I use is called MEDDPICC. Let me share with you how I came across this methodology and how it changed my life.

Imagine for a second that you are, at least in your mind, the best at something, and up to this point in your life, for the most part, you have been proven correct. That was me, basking in glorious ignorance. After all, I had already done some amazing things and had been living a sales career I was proud of. I had made consistent multiple six figure incomes, hit or exceeded plan every year at every company I had been part of, and won multiple Presidents' Clubs (a company's awards trip for top performers) to some of the best destinations in the world. I'd hired and trained people who had gone on to hit their goals and personally taken on initiatives that helped to shape the strategy and culture of multiple organizations. I thought I was elite. I thought I had this sales thing figured out. Boy, was I wrong.

At this point in my career, it was rare for me to really get pushed, and pushed hard, on my sales ability. After all, I was successful, working in a senior level sales role at a Fortune 250 company. But then came something that flipped my world upside down. I've read many books on sales, and as I mentioned in my other story, I've been trained by some great people and companies. After ARAMARK, I went on to CareerBuilder which has been consistently ranked as one of the best companies to sell for with the best training. A new leader was assigned to my team. His name was Gregory Donovan. At first, I took the approach of, asking "Who is this new guy and what can he do for me?" (As I get older, wiser, and frankly realize how stupid I am, I have learned that it's important to allow people to challenge me, and Gregory did like no other.) He had been a successful enterprise salesperson for years, started his own company and sold it, and was very well connected with heads of sales at some huge companies. He quickly showed me that I had much more room to grow.

Let me be honest - I think there are times in sales, or in anything, where you experience a lot of success and you get complacent as a result. You expect that your success will keep going, because why wouldn't it? You forget that to get where you are, you had to earn it, DAILY. Not only did Gregory smack that reality back into me, he showed me how much more I could be doing, and in turn, how much more I could be making. He quickly, and in a rather stoic way, showed me he was the master while I was the student. He painted a new reality for me that I had to achieve.

109

So, how did he shake my foundation? Oddly enough, it was easier than I thought possible. He simply asked me during one of our goal setting meetings, "How much money do you want to make this fiscal?" I told him, and it was a pretty solid number. He laughed at me, in a very encouraging way. He said, "You're better than that." I challenged him, of course, because I thought the number I had given him was a good number. I remember this moment, because a weird emotion hit me when he told me I could do more. It was part anger ("How dare you question me? I already do so much, what can doing more really achieve? What about the law of diminishing returns?"). There was also some fear in there as it made me think that maybe I wasn't as good as I thought. Honestly, I didn't believe him. I didn't know how to do more than I was and couldn't see how doing more would even translate into more results. With a very simple question, he had shone a bright light on a blind spot of mine.

What followed was almost a discovery session, like what we all put our clients through. Again, we were new to our relationship together, so he sought to understand everything I was doing (he already had some idea) and get me to explain my process. He learned everything about how I worked and what I did. At the end, as if he already knew the answer, he said, "You are good, but you can do more." I simply said, "How?"

Let's take a quick pause here.

I am going to leave you with some important things in the following paragraph, and I am going to get into exactly how to make some changes that will forever impact you. But more importantly, you need to be coachable. I am not the only one Gregory asked this information from and gave this information to. But I am the one who took the coaching and ran with it. I have always believed that if you want to be the best, you need to be open to learning. You need to be humble, to seek out people who are better than you, and to be open to getting a punch of reality. I would argue the most important thing a salesperson needs to be in their career is coachable.

OK, let's resume, "How could I double my income?" He told me some obvious stuff. It was clear I needed to prospect more, so he challenged me to figure it out. I needed to up my game with building better business cases, and push executives for data, alignment, validation, and change. This would lead to deeper discovery sessions, discovery that takes twice as long as the presentation to follow. But most importantly he would teach me a new methodology that changed my game forever.

This was called MEDDPICC.

So, what do these eight letters that will forever change your life in sales mean?

METRICS—What is the business case? Think of the hard dollars, real value, and improvements in KPIs that your solution brings that justify a change. This is an actual mathematical equation, not a guess.

ECONOMIC BUYER—Who can spend money, has budget, can CREATE budget, and can sign a contract?

DECISION CRITERA—What is their wish list? What items will you be measured on and need to achieve to earn their business?

DECISION PROCESS—Who is involved? When do they want to make a decision? When do they want to go live?

PAPER PROCESS—What is the legal process a company will go through? Who are the people involved? How long does it take them to review, redline, and give approval for signature? This is critical to learn if you want to make sure deals close on time.

IDENTIFY PAIN—What are the real issues, goals, and outcomes? This, along with metrics, helps solidify the "Why change?" message.

CHAMPIONS—Who will give you inside information and sell for you when you are not there?

COMPETITION—Who are they? What differentiates you from them? What landmines can you set?

All the above criteria are color-coded red, yellow, or green. Your job during the sales process is to get them all to green as fast as possible. Red is information you don't know. Yellow is information you know some of, but it may not be 100% validated. Green means you are 100% confident the info you have is complete and validated by the client.

Now you may be saying to yourself, "But this stuff is obvious." Of course it is. It was to me when I first saw it, too. But then I went back and applied it to the deals I was working on, the ones I had lost, and the ones I had won. My mind was blown. If you are reading this book and already in some type of sales role, I challenge you, as I was challenged, to pick a deal you are working on. Write out the eight letters and be honest with filling in the information. I bet you anything you have red and yellow all over it. How much is green?

Again, we are all at different stages of our sales development, but this will change your life. It will show you your blind spots. It will help you prepare for meetings. It WILL help you win more. It is a race to get these all to green faster than your competition. Whoever gets all this information the fastest, and in a complete fashion, is likely to win. Nothing is guaranteed in this world - you could do everything right and still lose. But using this methodology will dramatically increase your chance of winning.

THE SELF-INTEREST MODEL

Everyone is fundamentally driven by self-interest. We're not saying everyone is selfish, but if you're not answering their main question, "What's in it for me?" you're not going to get very far when you try to influence or change their behavior. Once you understand what someone's interests are, you can frame your ideas around whatever will get them most interested in buying into your change. Most types of self-interest are straightforward; you can make safe assumptions about them. Most people want the following:

- More money

- More prestige

- More security/comfort

- More autonomy

- More support/resources

- Less stress

When you apply this to a sales or recruiting process, you can better understand what people mean when they talk about abstract things like alignment, influencers, and champions. To close a sale, you need to ensure that everyone involved in your deal sees that what you're proposing solves some sort of issue for them personally and their organization. You want to close a deal because that means you'll get more commission, more job security, or a better opportunity to get a promotion. Do any of your prospects care about those things? Nope. How much time should you spend talking to your prospects about any of these things? Yup, zero. What do your prospects want? A solution that makes their job easier, something that makes them look good internally, something that makes their business more money, cuts their current spend, or mitigates their risk. The more complex your solution, and the more expensive it is, the more people will get involved (on their side and on yours), and the more types of self-interest you will have to understand and satisfy. Many companies will tell their salespeople to act like an owner, which is a shorthand way of saying, "Make sure that everything you're doing, saying, and proposing is good for the company, and don't be afraid to work outside the box to get things done."

To clarify, just hitting these boxes for everyone doesn't mean a deal will get closed. If only that were the case! You need to consider that your biggest competitor in every deal is the status quo. It's almost always easier to keep doing things the way they have been done in the past. Any kind of change is a pain in the neck and unless someone, and their organization, is *excited* about the future you're telling them you can make a reality, you're not going to win that deal.

TIME MANAGEMENT

Even some of the best fail to manage their time well. If you master time management, you'll always outperform your peers that haven't. There's enough content on time management best practices to fill small libraries. Here are the key takeaways-

From David:

- I do the biggest, most time-consuming tasks first thing in the day. The main reason for this is that I view my energy level like a battery - I have the most focus early and less energy as the day progresses. When I do the most important, big tasks first, the rest of the day gets easier AND I feel energized, like a weight has been lifted from my shoulders.

- I make a list. Lists are important. I also treat my calendar as my "to-do" list. If you look at my calendar, it's almost always full. It's simple - I plan my weeks on Sundays and my days the night before. I block 30-minute intervals for everything I need to do. Then I treat those 30-minute intervals like client meetings. I do that thing, at that time, and don't let myself get distracted. This ensures everything gets done. It works VERY well when I hold myself accountable for doing the task at the scheduled time. Any tasks not finished in the allowed time simply get moved to the next day and time slot available. I also keep sticky notes and a pen next to my bed. When I wake up with those great thoughts, or panicked that I forgot something, I write it down and tackle it tomorrow.

- Dwight D. Eisenhower, the 34th president of the United States, created one of the best productivity tools of all time - the

Eisenhower Box, a decision matrix that helps understand what things to focus on and when.

- Box 1—Important & Urgent—This is stuff that must be done now and is very important.

  - Do these things now—for instance, if a client needs XYZ information by end of day or your boss needs you do to something urgent, make sure you get it done.

- Box 2—Important & Not Urgent—This is most things.

  - For many tasks, it won't create problems if you wait a few hours, or a day, the world won't end, but you still need to get them done. Use your calendar to schedule times to do those things.

- Box 3—Urgent & Not Important—Delegate these things— figure out people to do these tasks for you.

  - When you're starting out, you won't have anyone reporting to you that you can easy delegate work to, but there might be people in the organization that you can still get help from. Use the resources you have available. A word of caution- you need to balance this with being a team player. If you're the one person on your team never cooperating, you don't want a bad reputation of not being a team player to catch up to you.

- Box 4—Not Urgent & Not Important—Delete this stuff

  - These are just about all your time-wasting distractors

We have written about how planning out your week can make a huge difference when it comes to time and territory management. You can also do this with flights for national travel. If you know you are going to be in a certain city, call everyone you want to meet with in that city, tell them you are going to be in the area, and book your appointments around the first meeting. Treat that meeting as your anchor point, and then build around it. This will save you future flights and all the time it takes flying around the country. Just do it! We wrote about this earlier on. But it is VERY easy to get distracted and to let just about anything get in the way of doing what you need to do. Doing what is needed is often less fun than doing something else, so try to make it fun: set goals, milestones etc. Take a big task and break it down into many smaller tasks, write those down on separate pieces of paper, then crumple them up when you have done them. The tactile sensation of ticking something off or crumpling it up can feel really rewarding and can create a motivation to keep going. But in the end, it's simple - stop procrastinating and get your shit done.

Lastly, know when to say "no." If you don't get everything done, it's your fault, no one else's. You can't tell your boss you missed a deadline or didn't hit quota because you did this favor for that person or were too busy doing these other things.

From Andy - I went the fraternity route in college (for those outside of the US and unfamiliar with the term, a fraternity is an invite-only social club common to many universities in

118

the US), and while I had a lot of fun and made some lifelong friends, it was also a lot of work, and I had to grow up fast to make it work. Our chapter borrowed a practice from the military, specifically that you weren't allowed to say, "That's not my fault," or "I didn't get that done because..." or any variant thereof. If you were asked about something that had been assigned to you, and that task wasn't complete when it should have been, the only acceptable thing to say was "No excuse, sir." The point of the exercise is to drill home the fact that for an organization to function, you need to accept personal responsibility for the outcome, and if something prevents you from achieving your goal, that's on you, too.

Speaking from personal experience, it's not a comfortable or fun practice to adopt, at all. It's natural for us to point fingers and place blame at anyone's feet but our own. It's hard to sit there and take it on the chin. But once you get in the habit of taking responsibility for your mistakes and misses, I promise you this: 1) you will make less mistakes 2) your colleagues, prospects, and clients will respect you more 3) people will be more willing to work with you because they can depend on your honesty and candor (and know that you won't throw them under the bus). You'll also have infinitely more productive conversations with your manager. Instead of skirting around a topic, trying to hide a shortcoming, or explaining why you couldn't get something done, you'll be able to discuss what happened, what went wrong, and how to either fix it or avoid the same mistake in the future. Also, if you ever have teammates or direct reports that rely on you, they will appreciate this straightforward style and you'll get much better results with less stress.

This should go without saying, but this isn't a get-out-of-jail free card. Taking responsibility for your fault doesn't absolve you of guilt. You can't let this practice become a crutch. It's great to be open and honest and take responsibility, but if you're making mistakes left, right and center, you're just incompetent and honest. No organization has room for someone that's consistently incompetent.

Your number one priority is to sell, hit your goals, and set yourself up to hit future goals. Everything else is secondary. If you have time for something else, great, feel free to do anything you want to do. However, if you are like most of us, time won't be in abundance. Make sure to prioritize, list manage, and follow through with the things that need to be done. If you figure this out, you will find time to prospect, meet with all your clients, and put together everything you need. Then the little things won't slip through the cracks, and sure enough, thanks to good time management, you will be closer to hitting your goals.

STRESS MANAGEMENT

Look, life is stressful enough … a life of sales is even more so. We are subject to more ups and downs than just about any other profession. It comes with the territory, and anyone who's lived this life will tell you so.

From David: I recently spoke with a former employee of mine who retired after spending 30 years at ADP, a Fortune 500 company, in a variety of jobs. I asked him how retirement was going. We mused about the deprogramming that takes place after 30 years of living a life of constant urgency. He had already lost 20 pounds, was eating more healthily, sleeping better, and working out more. He was constantly being reminded by his wife that everything was OK, that it's perfectly acceptable to move at a slower pace. We joked that he needed to move to the Himalayas and find a Buddhist monastery to seek Zen. But seriously, this is a VERY high-pressure job where, "What have you done for me lately?" is the name of the game. You can be on top one month and on the bottom the next. You can hit your goal to just have it reset on you next year.

I have struggled with this, as well. I married a psychologist and she does her best to help me cope. I tell her, "It's you, not me, become a better psychologist …" Of course, I am kidding … I am the one who is messed up. In truth, I was that way before sales, but my profession has not made things better. After my son was born, this weakness came to the surface and I've been focusing on it more ever since. My old coping mechanisms were in no way enough for the added stress of being a parent. I just wish I had learned some of the things I know now sooner. It probably would have helped me with relationships in and outside of business.

Understand the difference between stress and pressure. Some pressure is good, even though it causes stress. It allows for a personal sense of ownership and the urgency to get things done. If pressure is applied externally to you, stress is felt internally, and often projected outwardly on to others. How you show up and how your actions impact others are often a manifestation of the stress you're feeling. Think about how you feel and behave when you are on vacation as opposed to when you are on a deadline to get a high-value activity done. For an example, think of the stress of finals week. In business, every week is like finals week. There are always deadlines, goals, and activities that need to be done.

Some of the top causes of stress in the job:

- Your boss
- Prospecting
- Managing clients and the ups and downs of winning / losing deals
- Goals and expectation of management
- Forecasts
- Stack ranks
- CRM Updates

Sales is hard work. It can be mentally and emotionally exhausting (and even physically, if you're a road warrior). The experience of reaching out to potentially hundreds of people week in and week out and being ignored, hung up on, cursed at, spoken down to, denied for no good reason, lied to, or just laughed at - it's rough.

Having a good system to deal with stress is paramount. At the end of the day, we're fundamentally judged on our output and our accomplishments. If a bad call puts you in a funk for an hour, your productivity takes a hit. Either you didn't do the work you needed to, or the work you did was below par. What happens if your manager has a tough conversation with you? Or if you lose that big deal you were counting on for the month? Or if you have a fight with your partner?

As Forrest Gump says, "shit happens," and sometimes it's completely outside of your control. You're not expected to be a cold, unfeeling machine—far from it, in fact. But you will need to find ways to manage your stress, ideally in healthy, sustainable ways. Going to happy hour every day after work to blow off steam can be fun when you're in your early twenties (and we're certainly not ones to judge), but that will wear on you in more ways than one, and statistically speaking, it will literally kill you if you do it long enough.

With all that said - are you running for the hills yet? Again, remember, this is a rewarding career, you just need to find ways to deal with everything that comes with it. Here's a list of best practices we've incorporated into our lives:

- Positive personal relationships
- Get enough sleep
- Healthy eating habits
- Regular exercise
- Meditation
- Pets
- Hobbies that take your mind off work

Nothing groundbreaking here, likely a list of things you've been told are important your entire life. You don't need to do each and every one, but find what works best for you. Find healthy ways to manage your stress so that you can bring your A-game every day. Just like with time management, there are a ton of resources out there for stress management – find what works for you.

MENTORS

Mentors are people who spend time with you that have more experience than you do in an area in which you are looking to grow. The most important thing is that you trust and heed their advice.

One of the best ways to get someone to act as your mentor is simply to ask. Ask your boss if they have a mentorship program. If they do, it's a good sign, and they will help connect you. If they don't, ask your boss who they would recommend you reach out to, as there are often people who are willing to take new hires under their wing and support them. Most of the time, these are the future leaders of the business.

Mentors are an additional sounding board and resource for ideas and ways to learn and grow - this makes them very important. They will help shepherd you through the organization and speed your growth. The best way to utilize them is by meeting regularly either by phone or in person. Keep lists of things you want their help with and speak openly about where you need their help. The more direct and specific you can be, the better. This allows them to pinpoint the areas in which they give advice and direction. Remember, they want to see you succeed. They wouldn't be mentors otherwise.

Mentors outside of your business are often harder to get, but the best way to find them is to join networking groups and attend events. Then, be honest and transparent with people you meet about what you are looking for and why. People that are open to being mentors often do so willingly – they enjoy the relationship and being there to support your growth. They often don't see monetary rewards from this, but it is a chance for them to give back, support their own growth at a company, or build a support network for the future. They are different than a coach: coaches act in a mentorship capacity but are paid to do so. Mentoring is a more informal arrangement.

Mentoring relationships will come and go like any other. Mentors often won't seek you out; they accept the fact that they are there for you when you need them. For a mentor-mentee relationship to be fruitful, you need to engage with them regularly and bring meaningful topics for discussion.

Remember, mentors do what they do to help. Make sure they know how you have impacted them, and the results of the advice they gave you. This in itself is a great reward, and it's all most mentors are hoping to get out of the relationship.

MAKING MOVES

When the group we surveyed responded around their future career progression, two clear categories emerged: they either wanted to start their own business or become a Chief Sales Officer. There are career salespeople who want to stay as individual contributors, and never have to worry about the burden of leading people or managing their own business, and there is nothing wrong with that. The business needs these people to create stable high performing teams. If your goal is to become a leader or start your own business there are a lot of paths you can take. A typical path can be found below:

- Often people start as a Sales Development Rep (Hunter / Appointment Setter) or as a direct seller selling small-ticket high-volume solutions

- The next move is often either small business leadership staying in a similar division or moving to being an individual contributor selling higher ticket items

- Next comes leadership again in medium-sized businesses or moving to enterprise large business. This can take the form of moving on from local, to regional, to national, to global sales

- Once you have done sales and/or sales leadership roles in small or medium-sized companies, you may get the opportunity to progress to larger companies or deal sizes. This is where larger, more complex sales take place. You'll typically start making more and more money - the size of the commission follows the quota and the size of deals.

- The most typical path would start in direct selling, then move through managing direct sellers, and onto managing leaders, once you are in a larger company.

The size of your business impacts the speed of your progression. The larger the company, the slower the progression. But it is well known that if you are a sales leader at a big company, it can be the equivalent of a much more senior role at a smaller company, as the total business responsibility may be similar.

From David: For instance, at this point in my career I manage a team that generates roughly $10M annually in sales. This could be a head of sales at a small company, or the responsibility of a director or VP of a medium-sized company. My boss is responsible for closer to $30M annually, which could be considered equivalent to the role of a CSO at a medium-sized company, so the actual job title is relative. This means that, while career progression is often assessed in terms of the job title, the scope of the role and what you are responsible for should be your focus.

Self-Diagnosis

Before we get much further, let's talk about self-diagnosis - figuring out why you want to make a career move and if it's really the best choice. Usually, when someone is looking to make a change, they are either running away from failure or jumping to the next big thing. It's important to know which of these is happening and to fully understand your motivation to ensure you're setting yourself up for success in your next job.

Failure comes in many forms. Running away from it isn't always a bad decision, but it can be. Failure may mean you aren't hitting your numbers, you hit a plateau and don't see room for upward mobility, you don't like your boss or co-workers, or you just aren't happy in your job. If you're running away from something, the first thing you need to ask yourself is whether it is the company or you. This may not always be clear, but it's worth thinking about because if you're running away from yourself, you'll be in the same situation all over again at your new job.

If you're moving toward something better, ask yourself if it's really better or just more money, and if you're ready. If it's just more money and you're happy in the job you're in, you'll want to do your due diligence to make sure you will like the new position and company as much as you like your current position. While more money can be a draw, it's rarely enough to make lasting improvements in your satisfaction (unless it's the difference between struggling financially and financial stability). If it really is better, but you are not ready for it, you may fail and set your career back.

Your future employer will not be able to make these hard decisions for you. They see you at your best and need to fill an open seat to make money on an open territory. In fact, if they want to hire you, they will tell you just about anything you need to hear to get you to make a change. Only you can truly answer these questions for yourself. Below are some questions you can ask yourself to help you self-diagnose:

Questions about your current company

- Do you like the people you work with?
- Do you get along with your boss?
- Do you feel comfortable with the requirements of your job?
- Do you believe in what you're selling?
- Do you like the culture of your company?
- Are you satisfied with your company's treatment of customers and business practices?
- Is there anything else about the company or job that you don't like?

If your answers to the above questions (except the last one) are mostly yes, you are probably not running away from the company. If the answers are mostly no, you may be. Again, this isn't always a bad thing; sometimes it's best to get out of a bad situation. But before you decide to jump ship, ask yourself two things: 1) Have I done everything in my power to address these concerns? 2) Am I certain this would be different in the new position—have I fully vetted it out?

Questions about yourself

- Are you doing the required activity?
- Are you achieving your goals?
- Are you happy in other areas of your life?

If the answers to these questions are mostly yes, you are probably not running away from yourself, unless your answer to the next question is also yes:

- Are you getting negative feedback about your performance or interpersonal interactions? If so:
- Have you tried to correct the concerns, or have you responded in a defensive manner that puts the blame on someone else?
- Do you feel like you're being singled out, or are many other people experiencing similar difficulties?
- Have you heard similar concerns in other jobs or other areas of your life?

If you've been given negative feedback, have not tried to correct the concerns, feel like you're being singled out, and have heard similar concerns before, you should consider the possibility that it is you, and not the company, that's the problem.

Questions about the new opportunity

Let's say you've decided you're not running away from yourself. Maybe you're relatively happy in your current job or with your company, but had a new opportunity presented to you. Or maybe you've decided that running away from your company is your best option (it is possible to be both running away from something and running toward something better). How do you know if the new opportunity is one worth running toward?

- Are you excited about the product or solution you will be selling at the new company?

- Is the new job a promotion?

- Are there other aspects of the new job that are more appealing to you? (These might include the location of the office, the company's reputation, benefits, type of sale, what kind of training is provided, travel requirements, etc.)

- If there are specific concerns you have about your current job or company, will those things be different in the new position?

Are you ready?

If you want to run towards the next great thing, here is how you will know you are ready.

- You are consistently hitting all the KPIs of your role:
  - New opportunities opened
  - Expected close ratios
  - Goal Attainment
- You have won awards and been recognized by your leadership as a top performer.

- You are asked to take on stretch assignments or trainings.

- People come to you asking for advice on their deals.

- You have been asked to mentor new people coming in to the business.

- Your boss is asking you questions about your next step.

From David - Change can be a good thing. I have personally changed jobs numerous times in my career. However, they have also been for more senior roles, for better companies, better bosses, or more money. You notice I put that at the end: making more money is important, but if you make a change for just the money, and it is otherwise for the wrong reasons, you will probably leave a place where you have built a brand, put in the time, know the solution, and have enough time in your territory to go somewhere you don't have these things. If you do make a bad move, it will set your career back and affect you financially way more than the increase in pay would. Make sure you have closely vetted out the opportunity and that you are making the change for the right reasons, and it will probably be a successful transition.

Let me share how I ended up leaving ARAMARK, where I had been doing a job I really enjoyed. I left after 4 years to join CareerBuilder. I was headhunted from ARAMARK by a leader who would turn into one of my future mentors. As I have mentioned, I loved ARAMARK, but I had hit every goal, every trip, maxed my compensation plan, and frankly, selling uniforms, floor mats, and shop towels just wasn't getting me excited like it once had. He noticed this in me, and said to me, "David, you are great at what you do, but do you want to do that career forever? An opportunity with CareerBuilder will take you from the shop floor into the boardroom. You will get into strategic enterprise sales and learn more about business and solving big problems than you ever could in the role you are in." It was a good sales pitch, and I bought it. It didn't hurt that I also doubled my income on day one and I was selling digital advertising, which is way sexier than uniforms.

When I left CareerBuilder, it was to follow that same leader. The pay was at about the same level, but it was my first sales leadership role directly managing a team of almost 10 people. From there, I left to go be a sales leader at Monster, doing almost the same thing as before, but I was able to double my income again, and the move allowed me to work from home managing enterprise salespeople instead of those at entry level. From there I left Monster to go and work for ADP. At ADP, I went back into sales, but went to sell something I was passionate about and went on to have three of the highest grossing years of my life, before going back into leadership at ADP. This was also a long-term move, which could potentially position myself for a VP of Sales role at a large company or CSO role at a smaller one. This is because ADP is recognized as one of the best companies in the world to sell for. It's a highly strategic, methodical organization that really does cultivate the best and brightest salespeople.

Each move was strategic and well thought out. I took them all very seriously, weighed the pros and cons, and how those aligned to my long-term vision. In each job, I had a clear reason for leaving, whether it was solutions I was more excited to sell, much better companies, or significantly increased responsibility, all had good reasons and motivations other than money. They would also all offer me real growth in my career. More money was the icing on the cake for most of my transitions, but not all of them. Every move was for the right reasons and I was always running towards something I was very excited about.

What to consider

When evaluating a potential new position, it's important to have a critical eye. Make sure you are making changes for the right reasons. Usually, the only right reason is to accelerate your long-term career goals. This could take the form of a lateral move to a better company, an upwards move like medium business to enterprise accounts, or even moving into sales leadership. Don't make a change solely because the grass has been painted to look a little greener, because you lost a deal, or because of other minor emotional factors. Make sure there are real, concrete reasons. The grass is often not greener, and every time you start at a new company, you need to build your brand over again. So, unless there is real gain, it often doesn't make sense. On the flip side, if you notice your business is slow to promote people and feel you may get stuck in your role longer than you'd like, a change for a more promising career progression may be warranted. Unless you really love what you're doing and want to do it for a long time, it's all about moving forward towards that end goal.

Internal moves

- Is this effectively a promotion?
- Am I confident that the devil I don't know is better than the devil I know?
- Will this get me to my future goals faster?
- Am I measurably more passionate about the new job then the old
- How do I feel about my new potential boss versus my current boss?

How will you know when you are ready for your next job? Are you functioning at the highest levels in the job you are in? Are you hitting every performance indicator? You can't ask your business for the next step until you are hitting the objectives of the job you are in. When you think you are ready, ask to shadow and begin working with people in the role you want next. If the business thinks you are ready, or may be ready soon, they will gladly support this. Learn that job and begin demonstrating some of the key differences you could make. If people in the job above yours need to demonstrate better business acumen, get some training on the topic. If they work with larger clients, aim to show success at the upper end of your client base. If they deal with executives more, show how you are doing that within your business book. Once you have shown the person in the role above yours that you are competent, ask them to allow you to join them on calls, and maybe do pieces of the process. If you want to go into leadership, ask the business to pay for leadership development classes or to put you through a program if they have it. Or maybe you could start to run team meetings. You need to master the job you are in, then start acting in ways that clearly show you can handle the next step.

Your boss should always know your career goals. They should be setting clear expectations with you and discussing what you would need to do to accomplish the goal. These are important conversations you want to make a habit of documenting. You never know what may happen in the future in terms of office politics, or if, for instance, your boss ends up leaving. All your work may be lost without documentation on your goals, progress towards the goal, etc. Good bosses see their job as creating successful, promotable employees, because that is what is best for the business. It is a red flag if your boss does not act accordingly, but also bear in mind that it is your job to own your career progression.

External moves

Questions to ask yourself:

- Is this effectively a promotion?

- Am I confident that the devil I don't know is better than the devil I know?

- Will this get me to my future goals faster?

- Am I measurably more passionate about the new company vs. the old?

- How do I feel about my new potential boss versus my current boss?

- How do I feel about the culture?

- Do I like the work environment?

Bear in mind once again that it's not always about money. For instance, say it is more money but a longer commute, or you will be working for a boss that gives you a bad vibe, or in an office that isn't as enjoyable. What are the non-monetary factors worth as far as long-term job satisfaction? Money should only be a part of the equation. It's best to balance the short-term changes with your long-term vision - in the short term, money and job satisfaction and in the long term, clear milestones and career progression. If all those things align, it often makes sense to make a change.

Things to research about the position:

- The company's vision statement and long-term goals. This is especially important in smaller companies. (You don't want to join and learn they have a 6-month acquisition strategy.)

- Their competitors and how they are positioned in the market. (This will show you how hard it will be to sell their solution - the ideal option is to interview with their competitors.)

- How long are people in their positions, and how long career progression takes?

- Ask salespeople there for their opinion. Don't share offer details, but ask anything else about the boss, the culture, the number of people hitting their goals, what their loves & hates are, and so on. See if you get similar stories to what you have been told by the interviewers.

  - Most companies will let you go to lunch with a future co-worker. Do that, ask for real details, why they joined, why they have stayed, what they see as their career path and other similar questions.

  - Again, this is a way to establish the accuracy of the story that has been presented to you and culture fit.

- Read external reviews like Glassdoor and see if that aligns with what you have been told.

The Walking Fee

From Andy - There's a story I want to share from my time in agency recruiting to really drive these points home. I had a close teammate and friend, Keith, who was recruiting experienced engineers within the oilfield services space. While there are many, many oilfield services companies, at the time there were four major ones, and one of them was his client. Keith found a candidate and within five seconds of looking at his resumé he was excited. (On average, an experienced recruiter can scan and digest a resumé in about six seconds). And within the first 30 seconds of his conversation with the candidate, he knew he had a deal—a "walking fee," as we call them in the agency recruiting world—a candidate so perfect for the job they can just walk right into it, earning the recruiter a nice fee in the process.

The candidate had started his career with one of the major oilfield services companies, he spent five years there, then he had gone to another major oilfield services company, and he spent another five years there, and then he had spent yet another five years at another one. The only one he hadn't worked for? Keith's client. When asked about why he was looking for a new role he said it was time for a change— which is understandable after 5 years with a company. When asked why he was interested in working for Keith's client, he said he'd already checked out the other three, it was time for the last one—also understandable. After 15 years in the industry, he'd known about, competed with, and seen many of his former colleagues go to or come from this last major player in the space.

Now, I'm not Keith, so I can't say with 100% confidence that this was the easiest deal of his recruitment career, and I don't want to belittle the work he had to do to land the client and find the candidate – but I'd put good money on bad odds that it was at least in his top three. Normally in a recruitment process, the candidate's qualifications, skill set, achievements, motivations, and career history get picked over with a fine-tooth comb. Hiring teams are very cautious of making a bad decision, and for good reason: a bad hire is an incredibly costly mistake and can totally derail a team. Furthermore, agency recruiters typically charge their clients somewhere between 20-25% of the candidate's base salary for their service, so HR teams and hiring managers are even more cautious before signing off on hiring a candidate put forth by an agency recruiter. In this case, though, the candidate nearly had the job before he walked in by virtue of the excellent companies and track record he'd already established, removing a ton of uncertainty from the hiring team's mind. The takeaway from this story is that as you continue to build upon and manage your career successful, the transitions become easier.

Leaving

Whether you are leaving your team and making an internal move or accepting a position outside your company, it should go without saying to make your transition with grace. Your brand stays with you forever, and you never know who you may be working with again in the future. We've seen people who acted badly during a transition at one company being vetoed at a future company later in their career as a result. Remember, most people have 40+ year careers and sales is a smaller community than you might realize, so the chances of running in to people again are high.

With that said, here are some best practices:

- Give at least two weeks' notice. If the business asks you to stay longer or your employment agreement stipulates a longer timeframe it is fair to negotiate this, and work with them in good faith. They know this could affect your future employer, so it may be a delicate process. Be transparent with both sides. Seek feedback and a fair middle ground. You will gain respect on both sides if you handle this right.

- Keep it professional. Do your job all the way until the end. This doesn't mean you have to keep prospecting for new business, but it does mean you should transition your accounts to new people in the right way. Be upfront with prospects in cycle, and clients that you have strong relationships with, reassure them that they will be taken care of, and introduce the new representative.

- Make sure you map out any outstanding items and provide your boss with all updates on anything relevant. Tying up your loose ends and connecting people to protect your current employer will go a long way to help protect your reputation.

- Don't steal. This may seem obvious, but you may not realize that taking anything is stealing. This includes contacts, presentation materials, pricing books, and anything that is intellectual property, not just physical things like your laptop or that red Swingline stapler. Please heed this warning carefully. People lose their new jobs over stuff they took from their previous employer. Always do the right thing. The reason you got your new job is the good work you did at your current employer, so respect and honor that. You wouldn't be where you are now if they hadn't given you the opportunity in the past. At the very least, it will look unethical to your new employer, and how does that look on your "new brand."

Bear in mind it is a small world. You may move jobs and a few years later get hired back for a position at your previous employer with greater responsibility. This is another reason to transition with grace. Getting vindictive or saying that thing you always wanted to say may feel good in the moment, but the long-term risk is not worth it.

Best Practices and CYA Activities

- Write every email as if the whole world can see it. If it looks like you're being asked to put something in email you're not comfortable with ANYONE ever seeing, rewrite it. If that doesn't work, try to make it a phone call. The point is that emails get forwarded, so if you phrase something in a way that might have been perfectly fine to send to one person, it might come across poorly and damage your brand and career if the wrong person sees it.

- Everyone, from janitor to CEO, has the same job — make your boss look good. If you can manage that you're golden.

- If you think something may be wrong, it probably is, so ask your boss before you do it.

- Pretend you are the CEO and ask yourself "Is this best for the company?" Make your decisions through this lens and you will always come out on top.

- You should document via email any important conversations that take place, even if it's sending an email to yourself around a specific interaction. You never know when you may need some degree of proof that something important happened.

- If you don't get a response on something important, don't assume the other person heard you or got it. Follow up and confirm understanding and follow up on actions.

- Prepare for every client interaction and make sure anyone attending has prepared with you. Ensure you've aligned yourself with the goals and desired outcomes of the meeting.

- Romantic relationships in the office are risky. Many relationships don't end up working out, and those that end don't always end on good terms. Even if it's mutual, and for the right reasons, seeing that person every day, potentially with someone else, can hurt. The best practice here is not to date people you work closely with. This can be a real career killer, especially if it ends badly.

- Always try to stay positive. It's amazing how much negativity can spread in an office setting, especially in sales. It's such a mental game. If someone is having a bad day, loses a sale, or is just perpetually negative, then buying into their emotions will bring you down, too. I'm not saying you shouldn't have empathy but be careful how much you let it affect you. People love pity parties, and all they do is create a self-fulfilling (and self-defeating) prophecy for your business. This can be especially true of people that are truly toxic. Steer clear of such people. Leadership notices them and they usually won't be around long. If you see someone that disrespects others, argues with leadership, blames all failure on everyone else, doesn't take the job seriously … you get the point. Don't befriend these people, they will negatively impact your brand and your performance. The old saying, "You are the company you keep," is especially true in office settings. Surround yourself with the best, brightest, and most positive - it can only help lift you up and accelerate your own success.

SECTION 3 RECAP

In this section we walked you through exactly what to do to set yourself up for success in the early days of your new career.

Some key takeaways from this section:

1. Follow the process and methodologies the business lays out for you. Don't argue with them or challenge them, you haven't earned the right yet. For your entire career, seek to understand why things are done a certain way, try them for a fair amount of time, and until you have clear data that says something is wrong or you have a proven better way, stick to the program

2. Just do It., Don't think too hard about it, expect to fail, try to face your fears and just get out there and do the work. Everyone fails when they are trying something new, the people that grow the fastest fail more, fail faster, and learn as much as they can from it.

3. Align yourself with the best, watch what they do and copy them. Things like talk tracks, methodologics, approaches to prospecting and deal management. Finding a mentor, or shadowing someone that is operating at a high level and learning to do what they do will accelerate your growth. This will require you to get outside your comfort zone, be humble, be coachable, and ask for help.

4. Your early career, especially if you follow the advice in this book will be filled with opportunity. Getting a promotion per year isn't out of the question if you put in the time, follow the process, and hone your craft. Remember to be thoughtful in those moves, and make transitions with care. Those early days are like chess moves setting yourself up for a long term win.

Don't just think through the job you could move to, think about the next 2 – 3 after that, and ensure that if you are going somewhere it is for something you are more passionate about, has growth potential not just for a few years, but for multiple moves in the future, and maybe you can make more money at.

This section was all about what you should expect when you start your sales career, and how to ensure that you get off to a good start. Proper consistent execution, and a real understanding and adherence to the things we covered will set you off on a very strong path. Put in the hours, do what people ask you to do, find the best and follow them, and just get out there and do it - people who work hard, do the right things, and build the right foundations for long term success will come out on top.

The End – Or just your beginning

We truly hope you found this book helpful. We tried to pack in years of wisdom, research, and best practices into these pages. We believe that if you follow the guidance we have provided you will go into a career in sales with your eyes wide open, get the right job, and be massively successful in your career. We couldn't have written this without going through many trials and tribulations ourselves, and learning from many of our own mistakes. We hope this will accelerate your learning and help you avoid some of the hardships we have experienced. Sales has been very good to us, and our goal is to help the next generation of sellers see the reward this great career path can have.

Please don't hesitate to connect with us on LinkedIn at https://www.linkedin.com/in/davidlbweiss/ and https://www.linkedin.com/in/andyracic/, or to reach out directly to us via our website – http://www.salescareerguide.com/. We are always happy to connect with aspiring sales professionals to give one-on-one coaching, and to support their development in their careers.

Thank you for taking the time to read our book, and we wish you the very best in your career.

Happy Selling!

David & Andy

CONTINUOUS EDUCATION

In your early days in sales, you are like anyone new at something. Every action causes you to learn, and learning happens fast and furious. Failures are common, and areas where you need to improve seem countless. It's one of the reasons why most companies start people off with small, high-volume transactions. As you make hundreds of prospecting outreaches a week and go on 10–20 client meets a week, you learn a huge amount. It is like a trial by fire, and you grow quickly. For our gamer friends out there, you can compare it to a role-playing game where the more activity you do, and the more quests you go on, the faster you level up.

> *From David: I remember reaching a point in my career where I started to feel like I knew it all. I was lucky to have a boss who would constantly remind me that "Leaders are Readers." He also made a lot of extremely useful book suggestions. As discussed earlier, salespeople are agents of change. The first book I read really did open my eyes to the concept of Appreciative Inquiry - to frame conversations and ask questions in ways that increase the probability of someone being open to change. It didn't necessarily change the game for me, and it didn't give me a huge boost, but it did sharpen my edge. I learned that you reach a point in your development where you are no longer looking for massive leaps in knowledge, but instead looking for incremental improvements that make you stronger.*

You can see this as staying sharp, adding tools to the toolkit, and giving you different approaches or perspectives to solving problems. This allows you to see different points of view and have diverse ways of figuring things out. It's vitally important to your long-term growth to challenge yourself to continuously develop, and not accept that who you are today, or even who you are at any point in your career, is good enough. There is always something more to learn, and always someone doing something better or different than you that you could learn from. Remember that and actively seek out new information.

This is as easy as going to Amazon or Google and typing in "Best Sales Books" or "Top Selling Sales Books." You can do this on a regular basis to catch up on strong ideas you may have missed. We have listed some of the best-known books below that we've read and approved, but this is by no means the be-all and end-all of great sales titles, and in 5 or 10 years this list might be wildly outdated. However, these all have their own key takeaways. If you spent a year reading all these books, then at the end of the year, you would have all the theory it takes to become a top seller.

No one has a silver bullet. Developing a sales career takes a combination of years of experience, and many perspectives. You can see reading as learning from others to become a better version of yourself.

How to Win Friends and Influence People (Dale Carnegie, 1936) - The quintessential timeless book on positive human interaction. Don't let the title fool you, this isn't a course in manipulation, it's just simple straightforward advice that you probably already know on an intuitive level and would do well to follow.

SPIN Selling (Neil Rackham, 1988) — One of the foundational books that has shaped modern B2B selling. This walks you though how to build business cases and overcome objections using data.

The 7 Habits of Highly Effective People (Stephen Covey, 1989) — Pretty self-explanatory. Many of the topics and advice we give echo the habits outlined in this book.

Selling to VITO (Anthony Parinello, 1994) – The guidebook on how to effectively reach and engage with the right person at your targeted accounts.

*The Art of Learning (*Josh Waitzkin, 2007)—Josh became an International Chess Master by the age of 16 and went on to become a world champion martial artist. In this book he breaks down what's he's truly world class at - *how* to learn.

The Challenger Sale (Brent Adamson and Matthew Dixon, 2011)—This is a modern classic - the foundation of most enterprise sales programs.

*Pitch Anything (*Oren Klaff, 2011)—wrote one of the best books on pitching, owning a room, and controlling the perspective, or frame, of anyone. Some of it can be aggressive, but the practices are important to understand.

Scrum – (Jeff Sutherland, 2014). Sales is a lot about project management, and time management. This book discusses a methodology used in software design, but has implications in all team and even individual performances around completing multiple tasks quickly.

Fanatical Prospecting (Jeb Blount, 2015)—Half motivation and half how-to, Jeb covers prospecting.

Extreme Ownership (Jocko Willink and Leif Babin , 2015)– Lessons in management and personal branding from former US Navy Seals and Both a way to manage projects and a way to manage your own personal brand

Never Split the Difference (Chris Voss, 2016) – Masterclass in how to negotiate as instructed by a former FBI lead hostage negotiator.

*Closing Time – The 7 immutable laws of Sales Negotiation (*Ron Hubsher, 2009) – This book will teach you exactly what to expect in every sales negotiation and how to come out the other side a winner

The Lost Art of Closing (Anthony Iannarino, 2017)—Anthony lays out a tollgate-based sales process that moves the deal along and get the buyer moving in the direction of buying from you.

Gap Selling (Keenan, 2018) — Want to know what the best do to get deals done? Read Keenan's book.

Sales Success Stories (Scott Ingram, 2018) - Sixty stories from twenty current top performing sales people. Regardless of your level of experience, there's actionable insight here for every sales person.

Podcasts

Podcasts provide a never-ending, free source of useful tactics, strategies, and inspiration. There is a seemingly constantly growing number of sales and sales-related podcasts out there. Luckily our friend Scott Ingram published and maintains a comprehensive list of all the active sales podcasts out there. You can find it at https://top1.fm/sales-podcasts/

GLOSSARY

This section is meant as a primer for sales and business terms. Every job and industry have their own terms and jargon - the faster you get up to speed on what's important to your team, company, and prospects, the faster you'll be able to add value and close deals.

Account – The person or organization that buys or might buy from you. Often used interchangeably with Prospect.

Account Manager (AM) – Farmer. Sales person responsible for managing current clients. Main responsibilities are to retain current accounts and increase revenue from current clients. Sometimes also responsible for bringing in new business like an AE.

Annual Contract Value (ACV) – How much a given deal brings to the business in a given year.

Annual Recurring Revenue (ARR) – ACV minus any one-time / setup costs. If you sell a SaaS solution that costs $25k to implement with a $200k annual license fee, the ACV is $225k, the ARR is $200k.

Account Executive (AE) – Hunter. A sales person focused on bringing new clients. Responsible for getting deals/contracts signed. They may or may not be directly or indirectly responsible for pipeline generation (depending on if there are BDRs/SDRs supporting the AE).

Bonus – Money you earn in addition to your salary. Typically, as a direct result of bringing in revenue/clients, sometimes as a result achieving other key non-revenue generating results.

Book / Book of Business – List of companies are who your current clients. Occasionally used interchangeably with Territory.

Business Development Representative (BDR) – a sales person responsible for reaching out to suspects and prospects to create pipeline.

Business Development Manager (BDM) – Often an ambiguous title. Business development in the strict sense is a more general term, but in the context of sales it typically means someone who is creating partnerships so that another company can use/resell your product/services. For instance, if a company makes a software product that fits into a larger space, their BDM might reach out to larger established players in that space and create partnerships where the larger company incorporates the smaller company's product into their service offering.

Business Model – Fundamentally, how a company makes money. What do they do, and how does that turn into revenue and profit? For instance, while Google does many (many, many) things, most of Google's business can accurately be considered an advertising business. Google provides free services to consumers (search, email, etc.), but they make money by selling advertising to companies. Depending on how you look at it, car dealerships don't necessarily make their money selling cars – while they earn a small amount of profit selling cars, they earn most of their money selling car *loans* and providing service on the cars they sell.

Business-to-Business (B2B) – Selling to another business (ex: accounting software).

Business-to-Consumer (B2C) – Selling to an individual consumer (ex: homes, cars).

Business-to-Government(B2G) – A subset of B2B specifically around selling to government organizations.

Channel Sales Manager – A sales person who sells through a distribution channel. For instance, if a company makes a B2C product but doesn't have a retail location and doesn't employ sales people to sell it directly to consumers, the Channel Sales Manager sells to (or through) distributors and retail stores who could carry your product to sell to their customers.

Commission – Like bonus, but usually strictly a % of sales made. Legally speaking, it's treated differently than a bonus.

Compensation – What you're paid in return for your services to your company. Comes in the form of base salary + bonus/commission + benefits (insurance, retirement, etc.)

Compensation Plan – How your bonus/commission is calculated. If you do X, you get $Y. Can be as simple as a flat percentage of each sale, but can get complicated quickly (different percentages for different products sold, accelerators for selling many things in a given time period, etc.)

Customer Success Manager (CSM) – Like an account manager but more like someone who helps your clients understand and use your product/service. Not always judged on increasing a client's spend.

Enterprise – Large companies/solutions - the biggest of the biggest. Bigger than SMB.

Incentive – See bonus/commission.

Industry – What a company does. Companies that make physical products are manufacturing, companies that design things are design/engineering.

List – See Territory.

On-target-earnings (OTE) – Your total compensation (base salary + bonus/commission) if you meet your sales goal or quota.

Margin – see Profit.

Patch – See Territory.

Pipeline – Potential revenue you can bring to the business if all the prospects you're talking to agree to do business with you. Typically, over time, as clients/opportunities progress through their respective sales processes, the total pipeline shrinks for various reasons (ex: prospect puts the project on the backburner and stops responding to communication, you find that you're not a technical fit for the solution they need, budget gets reallocated to other higher priority projects, etc.)

Profit – Revenue minus cost. Different products/services have different profit margins, which typically impacts compensation plans. For example,

SaaS usually has a higher profit than industrial equipment - creating software once and updating it as need be is typically a lot cheaper than manufacturing machinery.

Prospect – A person or organization that might buy from you. A prospective buyer.

Prospecting – Searching for new prospects. Reaching out to people who might eventually do business with you, attempting to gain their attention and interest in the solutions you represent.

Revenue – The money clients pay your company for your products/services.

ROI (Return on Investment) – The ratio of money gained versus money spent on a project. If you buy a stock at $10 and sell it at $25, you have a $15 (or 150%) ROI on that transaction (ignoring any transaction fees).

SaaS – Software as a Service. Selling the software your company created on a subscription basis instead of all at once.

Sales Cycle – How long it takes to close a deal from start to finish. Typically, shorter sales cycles mean simpler, smaller deals and vice versa.

Sales Development Representative (SDR) – See BDR. These roles/terms are typically used interchangeably. There can be instances where a company employs SDRs and BDRs and they have different roles and responsibilities, but these are rare.

Sector – Specific area within an Industry/Vertical. For instance, Ford is in automotive sector of the manufacturing industry.

SMB (Small and Medium Businesses) – Non-Enterprise companies. It's a generally vague term that will shift from industry to industry – there's not necessarily a set definition between SMB and Enterprise. Your company and the market will determine what's SMB vs Enterprise.

Social Selling – Engaging with your prospects via social channels (often LinkedIn and Twitter) *in a social manner* to generate opportunities.

Total Contract Value (TCV) – How much revenue a contract will bring in over the lifetime of the contract. Typically used less frequently than ACV.

Territory – The accounts or opportunities a sales rep is allowed to go after. Usually organized in such a way to maximize the effectiveness of each rep. Common ways to organize a territory are geographically, by industry/sector, or potential opportunity size.

Vertical – see Industry.

XaaS - <Anything> as a Service. The XaaS business model is becoming increasingly common as once someone buys from you and you deliver value for them, they're more likely to keep buying. Selling in the XaaS model, the upfront costs and risks to buy are typically smaller than buying all at once, and therefore easier to get approval on. The list of businesses that provide their solution as a service is growing rapidly. SaaS was the first common one. Platform, Infrastructure, Database are common now.

ABOUT THE AUTHORS

Andy Racic has 8 years (if we're not counting the neighborhood lawn mowing and handyman business he started in 5th grade) of progressive sales and business development experience across the recruiting, human capital and HR technology spaces. During his four years at the industry-leading international recruitment firm Michael Page, he brought in millions of dollars in revenue having spent thousands of hours in front of or on the phone with candidates, hiring managers and recruiters. Andy is currently the Head of Sales at Tango Health, a software firm in Austin, TX. In his spare time, you'll find him hiking, reading, and playing video games way too competitively.

David Weiss has over 20 years of sales experience. From the day he sold his first computer to working as a sales leader at ADP, David has done many different types of sales. He has sold in retail environments, in factories (helping them automate their business). He has sold business data, uniforms, advertising, technology, and strategic outsourcing. Throughout his career, he has consistently exceeded goals at every company he has worked for and he has generated over $50 million in Total Contract Value (TCV) sales across his career. David has had the opportunity to mentor and personally lead countless new salespeople and had first-hand experience with many of the topics in this book. He lives in Texas with his wife Ehrin who is a psychologist and their son Ian.

CPSIA information can be obtained
at www.ICGtesting.com
Printed in the USA
LVHW021810030720
659692LV00014B/1819